MW00390355

FROM GRACE *to* GRACE

FROM GRACE

to

GRACE

The Transforming Power of Holiness

Mark R. Quanstrom

BEACON HILL PRESS
OF KANSAS CITY

Copyright 2011 by Mark R. Quanstrom and
Beacon Hill Press of Kansas City

ISBN 978-0-8341-2725-8

Printed in the
United States of America

Cover Design: J.R. Caines
Internal Design: Sharon Page

Library of Congress Cataloging-in-Publication Data

Quanstrom, Mark R., 1955-
    From grace to grace : the transforming power of holiness / Mark R. Quanstrom.
        p. cm.
    Includes bibliographical references.
    ISBN 978-0-8341-2725-8 (pbk.)
    1. Holiness. 2. Christian life—Church of the Nazarene authors. 3. Christian life—Wesleyan authors. 4. Grace (Theology) I. Title.
    BT767.Q26 2011
    234'.8—dc23
                                                                    2011034563

10 9 8 7 6 5 4 3 2 1

To Debi, my partner,
without whom I am half of myself

CONTENTS

So that he who is thus justified,
or saved by faith,
is indeed born again.
He is born again of the Spirit unto a new life,
which "is hid with Christ in God."
And as a new-born babe
he gladly receives the "sincere milk of the word," and grows thereby;
going on in the might of the Lord his God,
from faith to faith,
from grace to grace,
until, at length,
he come unto "a perfect man,
unto the measure of the stature
of the fullness of Christ."[1]

—John Wesley in *Salvation by Faith*

1
WHAT THIS BOOK IS ABOUT

In Joseph Cardinal Ratzinger's preface to the 1968 edition of his *Introduction to Christianity*, he retells the Brothers Grimm fairy tale "Hans in Luck." According to the fable, Hans was a servant who, after working for his master for seven years, requested his pay so that he could go home and visit his poor mother. The master granted Hans his request and gave him "a lump of silver as big as his head." Hans took the silver and began his long journey home. After a while, Hans became very tired of carrying the heavy silver and, seeing a man on a horse, decided it would be much better to ride than to walk. The horseman convinced Hans to trade his silver for the horse since Hans was so tired, which Hans did, and for which Hans was very grateful. However, when he tried to gallop, much to his dismay he was thrown off the horse. Fortunately, there happened to be a shepherd with a cow along the way who was more than happy to trade his cow, who could give milk to quench a thirst, for the horse that was difficult to ride. So Hans traded his horse for the cow and continued on his journey. However, when Hans grew thirsty and tried to milk the cow, the cow was dry and, furthermore, kicked Hans in the head. Fortunately, a butcher was passing by and was happy to trade his cooperative pig for the contrary cow. The story continues with Hans eventually trading his pig for a goose and the goose for a millstone, which accidentally rolled to the bottom of a stream while Hans was stopping for a drink. Hans' conclusion to this latest turn of events was that he was the luckiest person of all since he no longer had to carry the heavy millstone!

With that fable in mind, Cardinal Ratzinger posed the following rhetorical questions:

Has our theology in the last few years not taken in many ways a similar path? Has it not gradually watered down the demands of faith, which had been found all too demanding, always only so little that nothing important seemed to be lost, yet always so much that it was soon possible to venture on the next step? And will . . . the Christian who trustingly let himself be led from exchange to exchange . . . not really soon hold in his hand, instead of the [silver] with which he began, only a [millstone] that he can safely be advised to throw away?[1]

Regardless of the relevance of Cardinal Ratzinger's application to his tradition, I think the story has application for those of us in the holiness tradition. The silver with which the holiness movement was entrusted was the conviction that the call to holiness was a present imperative and an earthly possibility. This optimistic message, that he who called people to holiness could truly make them so (1 Thessalonians 5:23-24), was the holiness movement's sole reason for being. While I do not speak for the North American holiness tradition as a whole, it seems to me that we have traded our treasure for things of much lesser value. Today, in the typical North American holiness church, one is hard-pressed to find a strong message for the freedom from sin and finds instead a weak evangelicalism that celebrates a generic forgiveness for sins without a corresponding call to holiness of heart and life. I'm afraid that the critique of Richard Niebuhr (a mid-twentieth-century theologian) applies to us today. In 1937, he wrote: "A God without wrath brought men without sin into a kingdom without judgment through the ministrations of a Christ without a cross."[2]

There are, of course, many reasons for the demise of a bold proclamation of the possibility of holiness in the here and now, but it may be because we have neglected to consider sufficiently

- the relational character of a holy God who hates sin for creation's sake,
- the sinful condition of a fallen humanity,
- the expected future judgment of that sin,
- the consequent dilution of the redemption made possible due exclusively to the crucified and resurrected Christ,
- the incredible gift of God's Holy Spirit to a redeemed humanity.

To paraphrase John Wesley, since we are not identifying the disease, we do not know the cure.[3]

My goal therefore is to provide the reader with as clear and relevant an explanation of the possibility of holiness as I am capable of writing, which is intentionally faithful to the Christian tradition in general and the Wesleyan-holiness theological tradition in particular. This is an original work, but by that I don't mean it is a novel work. It is "original" in the classic sense of that word, because it pays attention to "origins" and so for that reason is not new. I agree with Wesley's observation that if a doctrine is new, it is not true.

But that does not make this work irrelevant to the present age. On the contrary, the character of the timeless message of the gospel means that while old, it is always timely. And I believe that the "old, old story" addresses well the issues facing contemporary evangelicals in North America. In particular, the holiness message is exactly what is needed to speak to the antinomian (morally indifferent) and gnostic (world-denying) character of contemporary North American evangelicalism, which effectively undercuts the mission of God to redeem the world.

This work is informed by over three decades of immersion in the written Word of God, which was demanded of me by pastoring one congregation in one church for twenty-three years. In an effort to be faithful to the biblical witness, I have chosen the argument found in the book of Romans as the very general outline of this book. Therefore, I begin where the apostle Paul does, with a consideration of the wrath of God. That would not have been my choice if I were to write a letter to a church full of people I had never met, but it is what the apostle Paul did when he wrote to the church at Rome. So, I will begin where I would prefer not to, with an exploration of God's judgment of sin.

It is informed by over three decades of intentional study of the Christian tradition—in particular, of the Wesleyan and North American holiness movements. My debt to this tradition will be indicated, in part, by the chapter titles, which are the titles of the relevant sermons of John Wesley. I am not summarizing Wesley's sermons, so that one could read those sermons and receive the content of this book, or read my chapters and know what Wesley preached. I am simply acknowledging my debt to, and my harmony with, the Wesleyan tradition. Wesley is not my only source, however, as the numerous citations from those outside the holiness theological tradition will indicate.

It is informed by my relationship with Jesus Christ and others' testimonies of their relationship to Jesus Christ, which will be revealed in the confessional nature of this work.

Finally, it is written with an abiding love of our tradition, which has called all people, without apology, to the righteousness of Christ and which believed in the power of God to accomplish it (Romans 1:16-17).

HUMILITY

2

THE GREAT JUDGMENT

"'Twas grace that taught my heart to fear" (John Newton).[1]

━━━━━━━━━━━━━━━━━━━ ◆ ━━━━━━━━━━━━━━━━━━━

In March of 1758, John Wesley was invited to preach in St. Paul's Church in Bedford, England. The invitation was extended by Sir Edward Clive, who was one of the judges of His Majesty's Court, King George II. According to Wesley, the crowd was very large and very attentive and many of those in attendance were officials of the court.

Wesley chose this occasion to preach on "The Great Assize" ("assize" is the old English word for "judgment"). In this message, which Wesley considered to be the best message he had ever written or preached on the subject, he called on those court officials in attendance who pass and execute judgment on others to consider carefully that God the Son, at the second coming, was going to pass judgment on them! He reminded them that everyone without exception was going to have to give an account of themselves before Christ, not only for their actions but also for their words and thoughts. And he reminded those who had the task of pronouncing persons either guilty or innocent would they themselves stand before a judge and be either acquitted or condemned. They would hear the joyful words, "Come, you who are blessed by my Father; take your inheritance, the kingdom prepared for you since the creation of the world" (Matthew 25:34), or they would hear the dreadful words, "Depart from me, you who are cursed, into the eternal fire prepared for the devil and his angels" (v. 41). And Wesley encouraged those officials to live in fearful anticipation of that future judgment so that they might be properly motivated to live holy lives. He considered serious reflection on the future judgment a worthy motivation for the pursuit of holiness.

The message was evidently well received. The judge invited Wesley to dinner following the service, and the sheriff of the county encouraged Wesley to publish the sermon, which Wesley did the following summer and which he included in the 1771 edition of his *Sermons*. This, of course, wasn't the first time John Wesley preached about the rewards and punishments that are in every person's future. Heaven, hell, judgment, and the second coming were all recurring themes in much of John Wesley's preaching. "The Great Assize" was simply his best.

Contrary to Wesley, and except for the occasional funeral sermon, I was eighteen years into my pastoral ministry before I ever preached an "end of days" or "last times" type sermon—that is, one about either judgment or the second coming, or heaven or hell. (I had to ask my congregation's forgiveness for that omission when I finally did preach what Christ himself had spoken of so often.) The reason for my eventual preaching on the second coming was my decision to follow the *Revised Common Lectionary,* which is a resource for pastors and which recommends Bible texts for every Sunday of the church year. I was growing more and more aware that my responsibility to my congregation was to preach the whole counsel of God and not simply what I was comfortable with preaching or what I thought acceptable to my people. When I sat down to create a calendar in which the primary claims of the Christian faith were addressed systematically from the pulpit, I discovered the lectionary, which had been in use in other church traditions for hundreds of years. Thus, my commitment to preaching the whole counsel of God as prescribed by the lectionary led me to discover that preaching on the second coming of Christ was to be an annual event. As a matter of fact, the gospel reading for the first Sunday of Advent is Jesus' instruction for careful watchfulness in anticipation of his coming again, which is what John Wesley had preached to those court officials in Bedford, England. From the thirteenth chapter of the gospel of Mark, Jesus says:

> At that time men will see the Son of Man coming in clouds with great power and glory. And he will send his angels and gather his elect from the four winds, from the ends of the earth to the ends of the heavens. . . . No one knows about that day or hour, not even the angels in heaven,

nor the Son, but only the Father. Be on guard! Be alert! You do not know when that time will come. It's like a man going away: He leaves his house and puts his servants in charge, each with his assigned task, and tells the one at the door to keep watch.

Therefore keep watch because you do not know when the owner of the house will come back—whether in the evening, or at midnight, or when the rooster crows, or at dawn. If he comes suddenly, do not let him find you sleeping. What I say to you, I say to everyone: "Watch!" (Vv. 26-27, 32-37)

Now, my reasons for not preaching from this passage or passages like this one were many. I had grown up listening to "end times" preaching of evangelists and had not appreciated how easily hearers could be manipulated through such messages. I had heard preachers predict the imminent return of Christ so often that I had become a little skeptical of his returning, at least in my lifetime. I thought that choices made to follow Christ out of fear were not the right motivation for discipleship. But mostly, I did not want to preach on the second coming of Christ or on judgment or on hell, or even heaven, because I was afraid that specific part of the message of the gospel would be offensive to people and therefore would not be received.

The problem, however, which I have already mentioned, was that I wasn't telling my people the whole story. John Wesley certainly understood that one of the minister's tasks was to reveal the wrath of God toward sinners, as his comment on Romans 1:18 makes clear. He wrote, "The wrath of God is revealed - Not only by frequent and signal interpositions of divine providence, but likewise in the sacred oracles, and by us, his messengers."[2] From my pulpit, however, I preached an edited gospel. I was presumptuous enough to think that I ought to be the one determining exactly what parts of Christ's message were appropriate for their ears; that is, until God spoke to me concerning that belief and its motivation. In a definitive and formative encounter in my study one afternoon, God whispered with clarity and force, *You need to be more afraid of me than your people.* At that moment, God revealed that I was motivated more by the praise of people than by my love for him, and in that short word of discipline, he reminded me that I was going to be held accountable, ultimately, not by my church people or denomination, but by God himself. It was then that I began telling my church the whole story of God as expressed in the authoritative written Word of God and reiterated in the creeds.

That message expressed in the written Word of God and in the tradition of the church is that God's character of holy love demands wrath toward sin, which is expressed as judgment. While that message may not be heard very much these days, it is neither ignored in the Bible, nor in the ecumenical creeds, nor in our particular theological tradition. The apostle Paul, in his letter to the church at Rome, for example, began his argument with these disconcerting words: "The wrath of God is being revealed against all the godlessness and wickedness of men who suppress the truth by their wickedness" (Romans 1:18). It should be noted that God's wrath toward the wickedness of people is not a minor theme in this epistle and that Paul returns to it again and again. After cataloguing all the sins that are worthy of such judgment, the apostle Paul wrote that those who do such things deserve death (v. 32), that God will visit his judgment on those who self-righteously judge others (2:3), that people who do not repent are storing up wrath for themselves (v. 5), that God is going to give to each person according to what he or she has done (v. 6), that there will be distress and anguish for those who do evil (v. 9), that the final judgment and expression of God's wrath will take place at the last day when God will make known all the secrets of men's hearts (v. 16), that the inevitable consequence of sin is death (6:23), that all will stand before God's judgment seat (14:10), and that every single person will have to give an accounting of himself or herself before God (v. 12).

This is a theme that the apostle Paul repeated in all of his letters. In his first letter to the church at Corinth, after identifying the people of God as God's temple, Paul wrote: "If anyone destroys God's temple, God will destroy him; for God's temple is sacred, and you are that temple" (1 Corinthians 3:17). In his second letter to that same church, he wrote that the goal for every believer was to live a life pleasing to God, "For we must all appear before the judgment seat of Christ, that each one may receive what is due him for the things done while in the body, whether good or bad" (2 Corinthians 5:10). The apostle Paul called the churches of Galatia to generosity and humility by reminding them that God could not be mocked and that if they lived stingy and proud lives, they would reap their own destruction instead of eternal life (Galatians 6:7-8). To the church at Philippi, Paul wrote that the destiny of those who were enemies of the cross was that same future destruction (Philippians 3:18-19). And in a second letter to the Thessalonians, Paul used perhaps his strongest language when writing about the destiny of those who reject God's overtures:

> God is just: He will pay back trouble to those who trouble you and give relief to you who are troubled, and to us as well. This will happen when the Lord Jesus is revealed from heaven in blazing fire with his powerful angels. He will punish those who do not know God and do not obey the gospel of our Lord Jesus. They will be punished with everlasting destruction and shut out from the presence of the Lord and from the majesty of his power on the day he comes to be glorified in his holy people and to be marveled at among all those who have believed. (2 Thessalonians 1:6-10a)

Of course, Paul was not writing to those first-century churches anything that Jesus hadn't previously said. As a matter of fact, it can be argued that Jesus' standard for judgment was even more critically penetrating than the apostle Paul's. A summary reading of the Sermon on the Mount indicates this, for according to Matthew 5—7, there will be judgment, not simply for murder but for anger, not simply for adultery but for lust, not only for how friends are loved but how enemies are loved as well. Jesus' expectation for his followers in the Sermon on the Mount is nothing less than the perfection of the Father's love (Matthew 5:48)! Later, in that same gospel, Jesus declared that all will be judged according to every careless word ever spoken (12:36) and by how faithful all were to works of mercy (25:31-46). It perhaps should be noted that the New Testament also makes clear that it will be Christ himself who will sit on that throne of judgment, separating the righteous from the unrighteous. Jesus was even willing to tell those who would reject his message what they would hear on that day. It would be horrifying to hear Jesus say either, "I never knew you," or "Depart from me, you who are cursed, into the eternal fire" (7:23 and 25:41, respectively).

Finally, the last book of the Christian scriptures contains the most extensive description of the judgment day. John's vision included this compelling revelation:

> Then I saw a great white throne and him who was seated on it. Earth and sky fled from his presence, and there was no place for them. And I saw the dead, great and small, standing before the throne, and books were opened. Another book was opened, which is the book of life. The dead were judged according to what they had done as recorded in the books. The sea gave up the dead that were in it, and death and Hades gave up the dead that were in them, and each person was judged according to what he had done. Then death and Hades were thrown into the lake of fire. The lake of fire is the second death. If anyone's name was not found written in the book of life, he was thrown into the lake of fire. (Revelation 20:11-15)

In light of the consistent biblical message of the judgment following Christ's second coming, it is no mystery why the church included in its creeds the clauses referring to the future judgment. In the Apostles' Creed, which is the most familiar of the ecumenical creeds, the church confesses that after his ascension, Christ will "come again to judge the living and the dead." The Nicene Creed states the same: "and He shall come again, with glory, to judge the living and the dead; whose kingdom shall have no end." It is no mystery why almost every denomination has an article of faith that refers to the judgment. The Church of the Nazarene's Article of Faith XVI, titled "Resurrection, Judgment, and Destiny," states:

> 20. We believe in the resurrection of the dead, that the bodies both of the just and of the unjust shall be raised to life and united with their spirits—"they that have done good, unto the resurrection of life; and they that have done evil, unto the resurrection of damnation."
>
> 21. We believe in future judgment in which every person shall appear before God to be judged according to his or her deeds in this life.

22. We believe that glorious and everlasting life is assured to all who savingly believe in, and obediently follow, Jesus Christ our Lord; and that the finally impenitent shall suffer eternally in hell.[3]

Now historically this has not been a very appealing message to believers and nonbelievers alike, regardless of its biblical foundation. In our day, in which tolerance is considered the highest of virtues, the idea of judgment seems regressive, even contrary to the gospel. To many, the doctrine of judgment with its promise of eternal rewards and punishments is, at least, archaic and, at most, destructive. In light of the explicit universalism (all will be saved by God's grace) found in some Christian traditions and in light of the practical universalism making its way into the evangelical tradition, the current situation makes it necessary to provide a short explanation as to why the wrath of God—which leads to judgment—is entirely consistent with the love and grace of God.

To start, the Christian confession that God will come again to judge the living and the dead is the strongest possible indication of the honor and respect God has given to people created in his image; it implies that people have been given, by virtue of God's prevenient grace (the grace that comes to us before salvation, leading and pointing us to God), sufficient freedom for self-determination (the ability and right to make your own choices). If God is holding people accountable for their actions, then they must have, through God's grace, the ability to be responsible for their actions. Conversely, if there is no judgment, then it could be rightly concluded that persons are not ultimately responsible for what they do and who they are. If there is no judgment, it can be reasonably concluded that people are victims of circumstances beyond their control. While it would be naive and irresponsible to ignore the power of genetic and environmental forces to affect behavior, the Christian faith, with this doctrine of judgment, rejects the simplistic reduction of persons to the narrow status of victims. As Richard John Neuhaus wrote:

> It is destructively depersonalizing to suggest that there is no right or wrong for which people are responsible. This is not to say that right and wrong are always clear and unambiguous, but it is to say that the most elementary respect for another person requires an acknowledgment

of that person as a responsible agent. We do that person no favors by reducing him or her to a bundle of compulsions and social and psychological conditionings.[4]

Thus, with this doctrine of judgment, the Christian faith powerfully declares that people, by the grace of God, are responsible for themselves and their actions, in spite of their fallen condition and the detrimental circumstances of their lives. In brief, God's judgment is an expression of the rightful honor and respect God has for those created in his image and empowered by his prevenient grace.

Along the same lines, the Christian confession that God will hold people accountable for what they do is the strongest possible affirmation that their actions are significant enough to God to warrant such attentive judgment. If God does not hold people created in his image accountable for what they do to themselves and others, then it might reasonably be concluded that he is indifferent to his creation. As a parent would express judgment toward the behavior of a child who is self-destructive or destructive to another, so God's judgment can be similarly understood. Just as a parent's love mandates appropriate expressions of disfavor to their child, God's love toward those created in his image mandates his wrath. A parent's love could be called into question if appropriate judgment was absent; so God's love could be called into question if judgment was absent from his love. As William M. Greathouse and George Lyons wrote in their commentary on the book of Romans, "God's wrath is the dark side of his faithfulness to his creatures . . . For God to spare them the consequences of their choice . . . would be to encourage them in self-destructive folly. God loves his creation too much to be an enabler."[5]

Thus, with this doctrine of judgment, the Christian faith powerfully reveals that what people do, and therefore who they are, matters to God. Judgment affirms the relational character of salvation. In short, God's judgment is an expression of his absolute interest in those created in his image and is an expression of his providential care for his creation. Judgment, therefore, is a consequence of God's character of holy love.

While the message that God's love requires judgment may not be heard very much these days, love and wrath have long been understood in the

Christian faith as complimentary, wrath being a necessary consequence of the holy character of God's love. Gustav Aulen, the Swedish Lutheran theologian, wrote powerfully of this relationship between love and wrath:

> Christian faith has from the very beginning expressed [the] opposition of God to evil in the strongest terms. It has well understood that, if this feature is missing or even slightly obscured, love loses its essence and is reduced to a caricature of real divine love . . . The radical opposition of the divine will to evil becomes then in the last analysis the opposition of divine love itself . . . No opposition to evil can be more decisive and critical than the opposition of love. It lies in the very nature of love that it must react against that which is incompatible with itself.[6]

In full harmony with the Catholic-Protestant-Wesleyan-holiness tradition, H. Orton Wiley described this relationship between love and wrath:

> Holiness then, is . . . a disposition or a nature which manifests itself in a love for righteousness and in a hatred for iniquity . . . The Christian position generally, is that wrath is but the obverse side of love . . . God revealed Himself in Jesus Christ as loving righteousness and hating iniquity; and the hatred of iniquity is as essential to [God] as the love of righteousness. Divine wrath, therefore, must be regarded as the hatred of iniquity, and is in some proper sense the same . . . which exercised towards righteousness is known as divine love.[7]

Thus, the Christian confession that God is wholly hostile to evil is demanded by his character. If God is holy love, then he must and will destroy sin for the sake of those created in his image and for the sake of his creation.

Regardless of our ability to appreciate fully the implications of God's wrath—which results in judgment—the testimony of the Scripture and the tradition of the Christian faith is clear: the destiny of each person is determined by the judgment of Christ. In light of this clear testimony, a prerequisite to renewing the call to holiness comes through a renewed understanding of the character of God, who is holy love, and who is, therefore, wholly hostile to evil, and who must and will hold people accountable. More specifically, if there is an anemic holiness movement today, it might be due partly to an anemic understanding of the holy character of God, whose love demands that he hate sin and must destroy it.

Incidentally, when I began preaching the whole counsel of God, which included messages on judgment, the second coming, heaven, and hell, instead of being put off by the messages, the church was grateful and made more hopeful. Indeed, one honest parishioner responded with one word. He simply said, "Finally!"

3
ON SIN IN BELIEVERS

"The essence of immorality is the tendency to make an exception of myself"
(Jane Addams).

◆

The previous chapter called for a renewed awareness that judgment, with its rewards and punishments, awaits every person and that this judgment is entirely consistent with the holy love of God and reveals the relational character of salvation. Evidently, how people behave matters greatly to God!

There will be some who reject the previous chapter's description of God's character as wrathful for philosophical or theological reasons, in spite of the church's clear proclamation concerning the matter. Others, however, will acknowledge the authority of the biblical and traditional witness to this truth; but, in a move every bit as dangerous, some will exempt themselves from being subject to that wrath. In other words, they will agree that "the wrath of God is being revealed from heaven against all the godlessness and wickedness of men who suppress the truth by their wickedness" (Romans 1:18), but, in their minds and hearts, that wrath is directed toward all those other people who are wicked. In short, God only hates *others'* sin.

Excusing oneself from God's judgment or, to state it another way, being blind to one's own sinfulness for which judgment is coming is a persistent problem for all of fallen humanity. It is a problem that Jesus addressed in several ways on many different occasions. For example, in the Sermon on the Mount, Jesus is recorded as saying, "Why do you look at the speck of sawdust in your brother's eye and pay no attention to the plank in your own eye?" (Matthew 7:3). Jesus condemned those who, being blind to their own sin, would judge the sin of others. Oswald Chambers wrote that the only reason one could see another's speck of sawdust was because one had a wooden beam in their own![1] And in the parable of the Pharisee and tax collector (Luke 18:9-14), it was the confessing, sinful tax collector who went home forgiven and made righteous, not the deluded, self-righteous legalist who believed he didn't need forgiveness.

The apostle Paul directly addresses this inclination to excuse oneself from judgment in his letter to the church at Rome, right after he revealed the character of God's righteousness as wrathful. Leveling the ground between Jew and Gentile, Paul wrote to those who believed themselves exempt from God's judgment:

> You, therefore, have no excuse, you who pass judgment on someone else, for at whatever point you judge the other, you are condemning yourself, because you who pass judgment do the same things. Now we know that God's judgment against those who do such things is based on truth. So when you, a mere man, pass judgment on them and yet do the same things, do you think you will escape God's judgment? Or do you show contempt for the riches of his kindness, tolerance and patience, not realizing that God's kindness leads you toward repentance? (Romans 2:1-4)

Because of this tendency toward blindness to one's own sin, the New Testament writers generously listed the kinds of attitudes and behaviors that warranted God's wrath. In the very first chapter of Romans, for example, Paul listed the sins of those who reject God, saying that because they did not seek God,

> They have become filled with every kind of wickedness, evil, greed and depravity. They are full of envy, murder, strife, deceit and malice. They are gossips, slanderers, God-haters, insolent, arrogant and boastful; they invent ways of doing evil; they disobey their parents; they are senseless, faithless, heartless, ruthless. Although they know God's righteous decree that those who do such things deserve death, they not only continue to do these very things but also approve of those who practice them. (vv. 29-32)

Paul wrote a similar catalogue of sins at the very end of this letter, adding to the list orgies and drunkenness, sexual immorality, dissension, and jealousy (13:12b-13). In almost every letter Paul wrote, he included descriptions of behaviors and attitudes that were inconsistent with the Christian ethic. To the Christians at Corinth, he wrote that the wicked—in particular, adulterers, male prostitutes, homosexual offenders, thieves, the greedy, slanderers, and swindlers—would not inherit the kingdom of God (1 Corinthians 6:9-10). To the churches of Galatia, he wrote that it was obvious which sinful attitudes and behaviors would result in punishment. He wrote that sexual immorality, debauchery, witchcraft, hatred, discord, jealousy, fits of rage, selfish ambition, dissensions, envy, and drunkenness were clearly sinful and would inevitably result in final separation from God. In Paul's words: "I warn you, as I did before, that those who live like this will not inherit the kingdom of God" (Galatians 5:21).

The gospel of Mark includes Jesus reciting such a list. Mark reports Jesus saying:

> What comes out of a man is what makes him "unclean." For from within, out of men's hearts, come evil thoughts, sexual immorality, theft, murder, adultery, greed, malice, deceit, lewdness, envy, slander, arrogance and folly. All these evils come from inside and make a man "unclean." (7:20-22)

The church continued this helpful tradition of clarifying sinful attitudes and behaviors subject to the judgment of a holy God. In the sixth century, Pope Gregory the Great classified seven sins as particularly deadly. They were (in no particular order) lust, gluttony, greed, sloth, anger, envy, and pride. In more recent days, Bishop Gianfranco Girotti, head of the Apostolic Penitentiary for the Roman Catholic Church, listed seven social sins he thought worthy of the same classification. They are (in no particular order) environmental pollution, genetic manipulation, obscene wealth, infliction of poverty, drug trafficking, morally debatable experiments, and violation of the fundamental rights of human nature.[2]

John Wesley was not the least bit hesitant to list sins unacceptable for God's people. To cite just one list of many, in his sermon *The Repentance of Believers,* Wesley said that pride, self-will, desire for honor, jealousy, malice, hatred, bitterness, envy, resentment, ingratitude, covetousness, anger, foolish conversation, vanity, and neglect of works of mercy, if not repented of, would result in death.[3]

As a matter of fact, and this might be where the holiness movement has most recently diverged from the eighteenth-century Methodist revival most profoundly, Wesley continuously called all Christians to honest recognition, and authentic repentance, of their sin. When Wesley was a student at Oxford University in England, he and a few friends met weekly for prayer and Bible study, which they called the Holy Club (and for which they were derided). They created twenty-two questions for self-examination:

1. Am I consciously or unconsciously creating the impression that I am better than I really am? In other words, am I a hypocrite?

2. Am I honest in all my acts and words, or do I exaggerate?

3. Do I confidentially pass on to another what was told to me in confidence?

4. Can I be trusted?

5. Am I a slave to dress, friends, work, or habits?

6. Am I self-conscious, self-pitying, or self-justifying?

7. Did the Bible live in me today?

8. Do I give the Bible time to speak to me every day?

9. Am I enjoying prayer?

10. When did I last speak to someone else about my faith?

11. Do I pray about the money I spend?

12. Do I get to bed on time and get up on time?

13. Do I disobey God in anything?

14. Do I insist upon doing something about which my conscience is uneasy?

15. Am I defeated in any part of my life?

16. Am I jealous, impure, critical, irritable, touchy, or distrustful?

17. How do I spend my spare time?

18. Am I proud?

19. Do I thank God that I am not as other people, especially as the Pharisees who despised the publican?

20. Is there anyone whom I fear, dislike, disown, criticize, hold a resentment toward or disregard? If so, what am I doing about it?

21. Do I grumble or complain constantly?

22. Is Christ real to me?[4]

Years later, as leader of the Methodist movement in England, Wesley continued this practice of examination by designing questions for Christians to ask each other. For those who took seriously the call to holiness, Wesley created what were called "bands," or what might be called accountability groups today. These very small groups of five to eight people would meet weekly for prayer and Bible study and would have to answer "yes" to the following questions before being admitted to the band:

1. Have you the forgiveness of your sins?

2. Have you peace with God, through our Lord Jesus Christ?

3. Have you the witness of God's Spirit with your spirit that you are a child of God?

4. Is the love of God shed abroad in your heart?

5. Has no sin, inward or outward, [power] over you?

6. Do you desire to be told of your faults?

7. Do you desire to be told of all your faults, and that plain and home [clearly and honestly]?

8. Do you desire that every one of us should tell you from time to time whatsoever is in his heart concerning you?

9. Consider! Do you desire we should tell you whatsoever we think, whatsoever we fear, whatsoever we hear, concerning you?

10. Do you desire that in doing this we should come as close as possible, that we should cut to the quick, and search your heart to the bottom?

11. Is it your desire and design to be on this and all other occasions entirely open, so as to speak everything that is in your heart, without exception, without disguise, and without reserve?[5]

Once a part of the band, they would ask each other these five questions every week.

1. What known sins have you committed since our last meeting?

2. What temptations have you met with?

3. How were you delivered?

4. What have you thought, said, or done, of which you doubt whether it be sin or not?

5. Have you nothing you desire to keep secret?[6]

Regardless of the relative benefit or harm of such examination, Wesley's insistence on this kind of discipleship practice reveals his awareness of humankind's tendency toward self-justification. In particular, his insistence that believers submit to others' examination indicates his recognition of the tendency of even Christians toward self-delusion and of the need for confession throughout the Christian life.

In the university where I teach, I ask students who take an introductory course on the Christian faith to privately identify behaviors, of which they are guilty, from a list that I provide. In a classroom of approximately one hundred fifty freshmen, I project this representative list of behaviors and attitudes the Bible identifies as sinful:

Anger (self-serving)

Arrogance

Discontentment

Dishonesty

Disobedience to authority

Envy

Gluttony

Gossip

Greed

Idolatry

Impatience

Indifference (to human needs)

Ingratitude

Jealousy

Lust

Pride

Resentment

Rudeness

Selfishness

Sexual immorality

Slander

Sloth (laziness)

Consistently, these raised-in-the-church students (after having some of these terms defined for them) are generally surprised to discover that some of these are even considered sins and are a little disconcerted to discover that, according to the Bible, they are therefore sinful. I believe, however, that this little exercise among mostly Midwestern adolescents is a fair representation of the attitude of our culture at large. The characterizations of "sinful" and "sin," as defining humanity's personal condition and how people understand their own behavior, are disappearing. The rationale is that, "it's just stuff people do."

This obviously has far-reaching implications for a doctrine of holiness. If behaviors catalogued as sinful, according to the authoritative texts of the Christian faith, are no longer considered sinful by contemporary Christians, then forgiveness for, and cleansing from, sin will not be sought after. For those who do not understand themselves as needing forgiveness and cleansing, Christianity degenerates into just another moralistic, self-assuring religion, which obviously results in people remaining as they are—in their sin. The evidence that this is indeed the case is deduced from any one of the contemporary surveys of the American Christian community at large; the surveys indicate no appreciable difference in lifestyle or practical worldview between those who confess to be Christian and those who do not![7]

This is not good news. The Bible makes very clear that God will hold each person (even the self-justifying and self-deluded) accountable for their sinful behaviors and attitudes. It must be acknowledged again that understanding every person as under judgment for their sin is considered by some to be destructively regressive and counterproductive. Regardless of the reluctance to accept a God who judges each person's work impartially (Romans 2:11), the Bible is clear: "For the Son of Man is going to come in his

Father's glory with his angels, and then he will reward each person according to what he has done" (Matthew 16:27).

To state more specifically what was concluded in chaper 1, the destiny of each and every person is determined through the true judgment of Christ, who calls everyone to a repentance that leads to holiness. If the letter to the church at Rome is a relevant guide, then the prerequisite to renewing the possibility of holiness must be through a renewed understanding of our *own* particular condition as sinful. Thus, the way to renewing holiness is not through redefining terms, or through any attempt at self-justification, but through honest confession of what God reveals to us. In summary, if there is an anemic holiness movement today, it is also due partly to a refusal to recognize the nature of our *own* sin.

4

ORIGINAL SIN

"Without doubt nothing is more shocking to our reason than to say that the sin of the first man has implicated in its guilt men so far from the original sin that they seem incapable of sharing it . . . Certainly nothing jolts us more rudely than this doctrine, and yet, but for this mystery, the most incomprehensible of all, we remain incomprehensible to ourselves" (Blaise Pascal).[1]

◆

Those generally familiar with John Wesley's theology might be surprised to discover what he considered the "grand doctrine of Christianity." Those who don't know might guess that it was his distinctive doctrine of Christian perfection. Another reasonable suggestion might be his understanding of prevenient grace. However, according to Wesley himself, the grand doctrine of Christianity was, without question, the doctrine of original sin! The reason this particular doctrine received such a privileged status for Wesley was because of its fundamental impact on every other Christian doctrine. As noted Wesleyan scholar Thomas Oden has written in his systematization of Wesley's theology, the doctrine of original sin

> must be presupposed in any effort to understand other essential Christian doctrines such as incarnation, justification and redemption. One who has no way to grasp the perplexity, depth, and recalcitrance of human sin, has little need to speak of Christ on the cross. One cannot get to atonement or redemption until one takes seriously the predicament to which Christ is an answer. It is a foundational locus of theology.[2]

While Wesley considered it a depressing subject, the evidence that he thought it most important can be found by noting that the only extensive systematic theological treatise Wesley ever wrote was on the subject titled, as might be expected, *The Doctrine of Original Sin*. It should also be noted that when the Methodists wanted doctrinal direction from Wesley, he gave them forty-four of his sermons. In at least thirteen, original sin was referred to specifically; one of them, appropriately titled *Original Sin,* was a sermon addressing the issue exclusively.

The doctrine of original sin simply states that people are inclined to evil by virtue of being descendants of Adam and Eve; therefore, everyone is alienated from God. The word "original" refers not only to Adam's sin but also to the idea that every person, from his or her own origination, has an irresistible inclination to sin. Contrary to the enlightenment notion of the inherent goodness of the human person, the Christian faith declares unequivocally that everyone, without exception, has been diseased with sin. In Protestant theology, this condition, defined as a continual inclination to evil, is called total depravity and was so called to indicate, not that every person was as totally sinful as possible, but rather was as thoroughly infected with the sin disease as possible. Wesley understood total depravity to mean that the body, the understanding, the affections, and the will were all compromised by sin. This idea that the human creature was totally depraved was so essential for Wesley that he considered rejection of it a denial of the Christian faith entirely! In *Original Sin,* Wesley wrote:

> Is man by nature filled with all manner of evil? Is he void of all good? Is he wholly fallen? Is his soul totally corrupted? Or, to come back to the text, is "every imagination of the thoughts of his heart evil continually"? Allow this and you are so far a Christian. Deny it, and you are but a heathen still.[3]

According to the tradition of the Christian faith, this is the universally agreed-upon condition of humankind, which is evidenced by the agreement of otherwise theologically diverse traditions and denominations.

For example, the United Methodist Church's Articles of Religion—which were a Wesleyan revision of the Anglican Articles of Faith—say this:

Article VII—Of Original or Birth Sin

Original sin . . . is the corruption of the nature of every man . . . whereby man is very far gone from original righteousness, and of his own nature inclined to evil, and that continually.

Article VIII—Of Free Will

The condition of man after the fall of Adam is such that he cannot turn and prepare himself, by his own natural strength and works, to faith, and calling upon God; wherefore we have no power to do good works, pleasant and acceptable to God, without the grace of God by Christ preventing us, that we may have a good will, and working with us, when we have that good will.[4]

The Lutheran Church Missouri Synod, the second largest Lutheran denomination in the United States, includes this brief article of faith titled "Of Man and Sin":

7. We furthermore teach that sin came into the world by the fall of the first man . . . By this Fall not only he himself, but also his natural offspring have lost the original knowledge, righteousness, and holiness, and thus all men are sinners already by birth, dead in sins, inclined to all evil, and subject to the wrath of God, Rom. 5:12, 18; Eph. 2:1-3. We teach also that men are unable, through any efforts of their own or by the aid of "culture and science," to reconcile themselves to God and thus conquer death and damnation.[5]

The Westminster Confession of Faith, from which the several Presbyterian denominations derive their doctrinal beliefs, has a rather strong and lengthy statement concerning the nature of sin that was a consequence of the fall. The most relevant section states:

2. By this sin [our first parents] fell from their original righteousness and communion with God, and so became dead in sin, and wholly defiled in all the faculties and parts of soul and body . . .

4. From this original corruption, whereby we are utterly indisposed, disabled, and made opposite to all good, and wholly inclined to all evil, do proceed all actual transgressions.[6]

The Church of the Nazarene's Article of Faith concerning original sin reflects this Protestant orthodoxy. The relevant portions of the article, titled "Sin, Original and Personal," state:

5. We believe that sin came into the world through the disobedience of our first parents, and death by sin . . .

5.1. We believe that original sin, or depravity, is that corruption of the nature of all the offspring of Adam by reason of which everyone is very far gone from original righteousness . . . is averse to God, is without spiritual life, and inclined to evil, and that continually.[7]

Because it is beyond the scope of this book to provide a thorough biblical justification for the doctrine and nature of original sin, a few consequential passages must suffice as biblical support for such agreement among distinct theological traditions.

John Wesley considered Genesis 6:5 to be sufficient for his sermon on the subject, from which the title of this chapter comes: "The LORD saw how great man's wickedness on the earth had become, and that every inclination of the thoughts of his heart was only evil all the time." The Psalms are full of references to the fallen condition of humankind, with the most familiar perhaps being King David's cry for mercy subsequent to his adultery, which includes these evocative phrases:

Wash away all my iniquity and cleanse me from my sin.

For I know my transgressions,
      and my sin is always before me.

Against you, you only, have I sinned
      and done what is evil in your sight,

so that you are proved right when you speak
      and justified when you judge.

Surely I was sinful at birth,

sinful from the time my mother conceived me. (Psalm 51:2-5)

The apostle Paul provided definitive justification for the doctrine. In verses familiar to even the nominal reader of the Bible, Paul quoted several of the psalms and a passage from Isaiah:

There is no one righteous, not even one;

      there is no one who understands,

      no one who seeks God.

All have turned away,

      they have together become worthless;

there is no one who does good,

      not even one.

Their throats are open graves;

> their tongues practice deceit.

The poison of vipers is on their lips.

> Their mouths are full of cursing and bitterness.

Their feet are swift to shed blood;

> ruin and misery mark their ways,

and the way of peace they do not know.

> There is no fear of God before their eyes. (Romans 3:10b-18)

Just a few sentences later, he summarizes what he had written with these familiar words: "for all have sinned and fall short of the glory of God" (v. 23). And the Evangelist John asserts this universality of sin in 1 John:

> If we claim to be without sin, we deceive ourselves and the truth is not in us. If we confess our sins, he is faithful and just and will forgive us our sins and purify us from all unrighteousness. If we claim we have not sinned, we make him out to be a liar and his word has no place in our lives. (1:8-10)

It is ironic, in light of the overwhelming evidence of humanity's propensity to sin, that this understanding of humankind as sinful is not universally understood, accepted, or believed today. The Roman Catholic apologist G. K. Chesterton's succinct statement concerning the matter is worth repeating: "Certain new theologians dispute original sin, which is the only part of Christian theology which can really be proved."[8] Because of the overwhelming empirical evidence of humanity's propensity for evil, apologists for the doctrine have oftentimes simply recounted the history of humankind to make the point. The apostle Paul did so, in the first chapter of his letter to the church at Rome, in which he summarily described the universal sins of his age. Augustine, in the *Confessions,* illustrated the doctrine by recounting his own inclination to evil. In the familiar and insightful passage recounting his theft of some pears, he wrote:

> I was willing to steal, and steal I did, although I was not compelled by any lack, unless it were the lack of a sense of justice or a distaste for what was right and a greedy love of doing wrong. For of what I stole I already had plenty, and much better at that, and I had no wish to enjoy

the things I coveted by stealing, but only to enjoy the theft itself and the sin. There was a pear-tree near our vineyard, loaded with fruit that was attractive neither to look at nor to taste. Late one night a band of ruffians, myself included, went off to shake down the fruit and carry it away, for we had continued our games out of doors until well after dark, as was our pernicious habit. We took away an enormous quantity of pears, not to eat them ourselves, but simply to throw them to the pigs. Perhaps we ate some of them, but our real pleasure consisted in doing something that was forbidden.

Look into my heart, O God, the same heart on which you took pity when it was in the depths of the abyss. Let my heart now tell you what prompted me to do wrong for no purpose, and why it was only my own love of mischief that made me do it. The evil in me was foul, but I loved it. I loved my own [damnation] and my own faults, not the things for which I committed wrong but the wrong itself. My soul was vicious and broke away from your safekeeping to seek its own destruction, looking for no profit in disgrace but only for disgrace itself.[9]

John Wesley, in *Original Sin,* illustrated the doctrine by retelling the degeneracy of humanity as recorded in the Old Testament. Others throughout the history of the Christian faith have done the same. However, one does not have to go to the ancient sources to indicate the truth of the doctrine. A summary reading of any daily newspaper should be sufficient to indicate the fallen condition of humanity.

For example, the front page of my local paper contained representative stories of fallen humanity. A story reported that a police officer was placed on administrative leave for domestic battery against a woman with whom he shared an apartment. Two brothers were arrested for disorderly conduct after a convenience store clerk refused to sell them cigarettes. An allegedly intoxicated woman was found lying along a county road suffering from several injuries and was admitted to the local hospital. Some copper pipe was stolen from a local business, a man was arrested for aggravated battery following a fight at a bar, and a nineteen-year-old woman was arrested for possession of drugs. This might be considered a rather mild representation, but it is representative nonetheless.

The international news reports more of the same kind of degeneracy. A front-page headline told the story of the postelection burning of an Assemblies of God church in Kiambaa, Kenya, in which the perpetrators trapped dozens of old men, women, and children, because they were of the Kikuyus tribe. Witnesses said it was difficult to distinguish the screams of the dying Kikuyus women from the shrieks of the rival Kalenjin women who came to participate in the slaughter. The front page also reported on the investigation into the assassination of Pakistani Prime Minister Benazir Bhutto and the more than three hundred people killed in the violence subsequent to her death.

Headlines from around the world—from any time period, from small communities and large—would tell the same kinds of stories, all echoing the same message of depravity. This evidence led Chesterton to declare that the doctrine of original sin was the only empirically verifiable doctrine of the Christian faith, and it was this universal condition that led others to defend the doctrine by simply reporting on the evidence at hand.

John Wesley knew that a proper understanding of the nature of salvation depended upon correctly understanding the universality and nature of sin. Just as a revitalized call to holiness depends upon the recognition of the nature of God as holy love, and therefore wholly hostile to evil, so the doctrine of holiness depends upon the recognition of the nature of sin, with which all are infected. In particular, three characteristics of sin are underappreciated in our current theological climate—and this deserves serious reconsideration.

The first and most obvious characteristic of sin is its destructive nature. This is explicit in Paul's declaration that "the wages of sin is death" (Romans 6:23). The representative sins of the news accounts mentioned earlier are perhaps sufficient to indicate the ruinous consequences of sin. Yet, one does not have to read the news stories of strangers to witness this inevitable consequence. In my introductory course on the Christian faith (with one hundred fifty freshmen), when illustrating the destructive consequences of sin, I have asked them to raise their hands if they know of someone who has been deeply hurt by sin. Specifically, I have asked them to raise their hands to these questions:

Do you know someone who was raped?

Do you know someone who was sexually abused?

Do you know someone who was physically abused?

Do you know someone whose parents are divorced?

Do you know someone who is addicted to alcohol or drugs?

Do you know someone who is a purveyor of pornography?

Do you know someone who has had an abortion?

Do you know someone who has been a victim of a violent crime?

Do you know someone in jail?

One would hope that few of these young people—most of whom were raised in the relative protection of Christian homes—would answer positively to these questions. However, on almost every question, a majority of the students raise their hands so that by the end of the questioning, there are precious few students who had not identified themselves as having witnessed multiple occasions of the destructive nature of sin. I conclude this particular exercise with a final request. I ask them to raise their hands if they have ever personally suffered from the destructive consequences of sin. Sadly, and as might be expected, there is always a unanimous response in the positive. This universal suffering from the tragic consequence of sin is poignantly expressed by the apostle Paul with the words, "the whole creation has been groaning as in the pains of childbirth right up to the present time" (Romans 8:22).

A second characteristic of sin, and perhaps the most insidious, is its delusive or deceitful nature. This deceptive character of sin is skillfully revealed in the Genesis account with the serpent lying to Adam and Eve concerning the consequences of eating the forbidden fruit. The writer poetically records that "the fruit of the tree was good for food and pleasing to the eye, and also desirable for gaining wisdom" (Genesis 3:6). In short, sin presents itself as a good. Sin's ability to destroy is therefore attributed to its deceptive character. In short, total depravity has affected humanity's ability to even recognize sin as sin.

The apostle Paul wrote of this inability of the fallen human to recognize sin as sin in the first chapter of the book of Romans. He wrote that while God was, at one time, able to be known by men, because of sin, "their thinking became futile and their foolish hearts were darkened. Although they claimed to be wise, they became fools" (Romans 1:21*b*-22). In an earlier letter to the church at Corinth, Paul was even clearer concerning the matter, for he wrote using the language of Jesus in the Gospels: "The god of this age has blinded the minds of unbelievers, so that they cannot see the light of the gospel of the glory of Christ" (2 Corinthians 4:4).

This is why the deceitful nature of sin is so damaging. Sin woos with deceitful promises of life but rewards with the destructive consequences of death. It is every pastor's experience to hear the laments of people who were so deceived, echoing the words of Cain suffering the grievous consequences of his sin: "My punishment is greater than I can bear" (Genesis 4:13, KJV). People who suffer from their self-inflicted sin wounds confess that, had they known the inevitably destructive outcome, they would have never allowed themselves to be deceived.

The third characteristic of sin is the most important and needs serious attention: its power to enslave. Diverse theological traditions unanimously agree that people are "inclined to sin and that continually," and this is due to the corruption of the human being. However, the consequence of this corruption results in the individual being powerless before sin. The United Methodist Article of Faith (no one "can turn and prepare oneself . . . to faith"), the Westminster Catechism (people are "utterly indisposed [and] disabled"), and the article of the Lutheran Church Missouri Synod (people are "unable, through any efforts of their own . . . to reconcile themselves to God") all speak to the impotence of the human creature before the overwhelming power of sin. Humanity, by virtue of depravity, is in bondage to sin.

This understanding of sin as an oppressive power is revealed in Romans 3:9. Paul writes that "Jews and Gentiles alike are all under sin"; however, an alternative and more accurate translation in the NRSV reads: "all, both Jews and Greeks, are under the power of sin." The very familiar passage in

Romans in which Paul confesses the impossibility of doing good, indicates without question that sin is an enslaving power:

> I do not understand what I do. For what I want to do I do not do, but what I hate I do. And if I do what I do not want to do, I agree that the law is good. As it is, it is no longer I myself who do it, but it is sin living in me. I know that nothing good lives in me, that is, in my sinful nature. For I have the desire to do what is good, but I cannot carry it out. For what I do is not the good I want to do; no, the evil I do not want to do—this I keep on doing. Now if I do what I do not want to do, it is no longer I who do it, but it is sin living in me that does it. (Romans 7:15-20)

This particular passage is universally relevant and the reader can easily identify with it. The reason it is well known is due to the fact that everyone has a personal particular story of the good he or she is unable to do and the sin he or she can't help doing.

Those familiar with the theology of the holiness tradition recognize that understanding sin as enslaving deviates from the usual definition of sin. The holiness tradition has emphasized Wesley's particular definition of sin as a "willful transgression of a known law" and has generally neglected his more comprehensive understanding of sin as a disease that has infected all of humanity. In the holiness tradition, sin is understood as being a matter of the will. People sin, not because they are inclined to and can't help themselves—people sin because they simply decide to. This has not been helpful. Because of that too narrow and certainly incomplete definition of sin as willful transgression, the call to holiness easily degenerated into a call to submission to a multitude of legalisms. Holiness was not defined in terms of restored relationship; holiness became moralistic. Subsequently, the call to holiness focused more on someone's responsibility than on God's empowering grace. Holiness was a work, not a gift. People didn't need to be rescued . . . they needed to be resolved!

Every now and then, a young person visits my office for help in overcoming—to use the psychological term, an "addiction," to or the biblical term "enslavement" to—pornography. My counsel to students addicted or enslaved to pornography is the same as the counsel given by AA to alcoholics. According to Alcoholics Anonymous, the first of twelve steps to be freed from this addiction is admitting powerlessness over alcohol and acknowledging that life had, consequently, become unmanageable. Typically, when I ask students struggling with pornography if they can decide to simply stop, they answer in the affirmative. They initially believe that the issue is a matter of inadequate willpower and are usually simply seeking to be held accountable to strengthen their will. My job is to convince them that they have no power over this and that they are indeed enslaved to pornography. I tell them that if they truly want to be freed, they must begin by admitting that if they are alone with the material available, they will inevitably succumb. It is not a matter of will. It is a matter of power. They can't will themselves to be free, no matter how hard they try. After they acknowledge this enslavement, I ask them to confess their need of a power greater than themselves. For these young Christians, that "power greater than themselves" *is* Christ. It is only when they begin looking outside themselves for salvation that they are liberated.

Sin is not simply a matter of the will. Sin is a condition of the human creature. It is a disease that needs a cure. Understanding sin as destructive, deceitful, and debilitating, where everyone—without exception—is inclined to evil and that continually, leads to one inescapable conclusion: we desperately need an intervention. In short, the infection of original sin, which leads to willful sin, means that all are alienated from God, subject to his judgment, and absolutely helpless before it.

Thus, in addition to recognizing that God is holy and must destroy sin for love's sake, and in addition to understanding our own particular condition as sinful, a prerequisite to a renewal of the possibility of holiness must include a renewed appreciation of humanity's helplessness before the enslaving power of sin. It must include a renewed appreciation for the source of our salvation, which is Christ himself. To paraphrase Wesley again, we cannot know the cure if we do not know the disease.[10]

5

THE LORD OUR RIGHTEOUSNESS

"Mankind, that had fallen into captivity, is now by God's mercy delivered out of
the power of them that held them in bondage. God had mercy upon His creation,
and bestowed upon them a new salvation through His Word, that is, Christ,
so that men might learn by experience that they cannot attain to incorruption
of themselves, but by God's grace only" (Irenaeus in *Against Heresies*).[1]

◆

A young lady new to our church and brand-new to Christianity asked if
she could talk to me about something that was bothering her. After making
an appointment with the church secretary, she came to discuss her problem.
She was fairly nervous, but I supposed it was because she had never talked
to a pastor before. Our church was the first church she had ever attended.
She began by telling me she was very unhappy in her new marriage and
didn't know what to do about it. I asked her to describe the circumstances
of the marriage and what was causing her unhappiness. She told me she
was unhappy because it wasn't her choice to get married. She married her
husband only because she was pregnant with his baby and felt obligated to
her child and the child's father. She was now regretting that decision, feeling
it had been coerced by the circumstances.

While not wanting to deny her perspective, I suggested that perhaps
she was feeling more trapped now than she had at the time and that having
second thoughts about marriage was not that unusual even in the best of
circumstances. I pointed out that there were other options she could have
chosen than getting married. She could have chosen to raise the child alone,
as many moms do. She could have given her child up for adoption. Some
women even choose abortion over marriage. My intention was to show her
the other options people choose, not to advocate any of them. I just was
suggesting that since she had decided to get married in this less-than-best

possible situation, she may have wanted to be with the father of the baby at some level after all.

As might be expected, she rejected the abortion option. She said she never would have aborted the baby. So I said that I hoped she hadn't interpreted my mentioning abortion as an option because I thought she should or even would have done that. I was just reminding her that perhaps she wasn't as trapped as she had thought she was. But she was insistent. Over and over again, she repeated that she would not have aborted the baby, and finished with, "I couldn't do that . . . again."

I then realized that what was bothering her was more than an unhappy marriage. So I asked her if her abortion is what she really came to talk about. It was, and in the course of the subsequent conversation, I learned that she knew her aborted baby's gender, she knew the baby's birthday, and she even knew the baby's name. She had named the child she had aborted! And she had been living with the secret guilt and private shame ever since, never confessing what she had done to anyone. Her guilt and shame were so great that in the course of the conversation, she told me she was certain she could never go to heaven because people who do what she did didn't deserve to. She then added, with tears flowing down her cheeks, that she could never go to heaven because she couldn't bear to see the child she had killed.

I have since learned that this confession is not unusual for women who have had an abortion and that many fathers and mothers name their aborted babies, know their babies' birthdays, and fear the day they might see them again in the coming kingdom. In my role as pastor, I have listened to more than one confess the same story of living with the overwhelming guilt and shame of abortion in details remarkably similar to the one above.

And what could I tell her? There was nothing she could do about what she had done. No restitution was possible. She could not bring her baby back to life. She was helpless before her sin. The wrath of God that the apostle Paul wrote about in Romans 1 was a living reality for her. The sin the apostle Paul wrote about in Romans 2 and 3 was sin that was always before her. More than anything else, she knew she deserved God's righteous judgment. She deserved the ultimate punishment. And had I spoken about these matters to her, I would have been simply naming what she already knew.

I can write what I didn't say. I didn't say that her child was simply fetal tissue and that the abortion procedure was similar to having an appendix removed. If I had said that, I would have profaned the memory of her child and been dismissive of her pain. Furthermore, society had already told her that message, which she believed until the moment of the abortion.

I did not tell her that God didn't really condemn abortion. I did not tell her that extenuating circumstances made the abortion acceptable. I did not in any way dismiss the gravity of her sin. That, too, would have profaned the memory and person of her child, dismissed her pain, and disrespected her as a person.

So I told her what the apostle Paul wrote in Romans 3:21. I told her God had made provision for her in the person of Jesus Christ. Christ had sacrificed his life for hers and taken the punishment that she deserved. I told her God had atoned for her sin, the sin for which she could do nothing.

The apostle Paul, after writing of the sin that had so thoroughly infected and incapacitated the human race, so that all persons without exception were helpless to save themselves, wrote of what God had done for his fallen creation. Beginning with the understated words, *"But now,"* which indicate a change of direction in his letter, Paul wrote:

> But now a righteousness from God, apart from law, has been made known, to which the Law and the Prophets testify. This righteousness from God comes through faith in Jesus Christ to all who believe. There is no difference, for all have sinned and fall short of the glory of God, and are justified freely by his grace through the redemption that came by Christ Jesus. God presented him as a sacrifice of atonement, through faith in his blood. He did this to demonstrate his justice, because in his forbearance he had left the sins committed beforehand unpunished—he did it to demonstrate his justice at the present time, so as to be just and the one who justifies those who have faith in Jesus. (Romans 3:21-26)

According to the Scriptures, God has graciously intervened to save his creation from sin. No amount of human self-effort, no matter how diligent, could provide sufficient justification for such wickedness. The only hope for humanity was for God to intervene, and in that profound passage from Romans, the apostle Paul summarizes the good news. Those who, in trusting faith, embrace the gospel are made righteous by virtue of Jesus Christ's sacrifice on the cross. God, through Jesus Christ's voluntary sacrifice, saves people helpless to save themselves. The Scriptures and Christian tradition teach that without the cross, humanity would have been forever alienated from God, forever enslaved to sin, forever subject to judgment, and forever ultimately lost.

This gracious intervention was, however, costly. While the apostle Paul, in Romans 3:24, uses the word "freely" to characterize the nature of justification, it obviously wasn't "free" from God's perspective. Reconciliation between God and humanity cost God the death of his Son.

This is difficult to fully comprehend; much ink and, ironically, much blood has been spilled over how to interpret the atonement. Wesley recommended humility when expounding on the significance of Christ's death:

It is true that I can no more comprehend it than . . . perhaps I might say, than the angels of God, than the highest created understanding. Our reason is here quickly bewildered. If we attempt to [elaborate] in this field, we find no end, in wandering mazes lost.[2]

However, the death of Christ on the cross has been understood to reveal important and definitive aspects of the character of God and nature of salvation.

At the very least, or maybe at the very most, the death of Christ on the cross reveals the extravagant and sacrificial love of God. The cross of Christ is the ultimate evidence of God's love for humanity and it defines the nature of that love. Jesus himself provided us with the language to understand his sacrifice; on the night of his betrayal, he said, "Greater love has no one than this, that he lay down his life for his friends" (John 15:13).

The concept of the cross revealing God's love is so commonly understood today that we risk this truth becoming mundane. However, serious reflection on the cross as evidence of the extent of God's love can be truly transformative. The apostle Paul wrote of the transforming power of the cross in his letter to the church at Corinth. He wrote:

If we are out of our mind, it is for the sake of God; if we are in our right mind, it is for you. For *Christ's love compels us,* because we are convinced that one died for all, and therefore all died. And he died for all, that those who live should no longer live for themselves but for him who died for them and was raised again. (2 Corinthians 5:13-15, emphasis added)

This understanding of the cross as revealing the love of God so compellingly that it had the power to overcome sin was suggested most famously by the twelfth-century French scholastic theologian Peter Abelard, whose theory of atonement is known as the moral influence theory. A millennium ago, he wrote in his commentary on the Epistle to the Romans:

Love is increased by the faith which we have concerning Christ because . . . by suffering . . . He has demonstrated to us that supreme love of which Christ himself speaks: "Greater love has no one than this . . ." As a result, our hearts should be set on fire by such a gift of divine grace, and true love should not hold back from suffering anything for his sake . . . Therefore, our redemption through the suffering of Christ is that deeper love within us which not only frees us from slavery to sin, but also secures for us the true liberty of the children of God, in order that we might do all things out of love rather than out of fear—love for him who has shown us such grace that no greater can be found.[3]

The cross as revealing the power of the love of God is beautifully penned in the hymn of Charles Wesley "And Can It Be?" While John and Charles Wesley did not believe that the moral influence theory was sufficient to understand the atonement, they understood the motivating power of the cross. Charles wrote:

> And can it be that I should gain
> An interest in the Savior's blood?
> Died He for me, who caused His pain—
> For me, who Him to death pursued?
> Amazing love! How can it be,
> That Thou, my God, shouldst die for me?

He left His Father's throne above
   So free, so infinite His grace—
Emptied Himself of all but love,
   And bled for Adam's helpless race:
'Tis mercy all, immense and free,
For O my God, it found out me!

Long my imprisoned spirit lay,
   Fast bound in sin and nature's night;
Thine eye diffused a quickening ray—I woke,
   the dungeon flamed with light;
My chains fell off, my heart was free.
I rose, went forth, and followed Thee.

No condemnation now I dread;
   Jesus, and all in Him, is mine;
Alive in Him, my living Head,
   And clothed in righteousness divine,
Bold I approach th'eternal throne,
And claim the crown, through Christ my own.[4]

The love of God revealed in the cross is able to overcome the alienation between God and man; this love's power persuades people that their sins are forgiven, provides assurance of God's continued favor, and promises eternal blessedness. Thus, at the very least—or most—the death of Christ on the cross reveals the extravagant love of God and the sacrificial nature of that love.

However, this very familiar understanding of Christ's life and death as revealing God's love does not exhaust the church's understanding of the atonement. One of the earliest atonement theories—known as the "classical" or *Christus Victor* theory—understood the cross of Christ as a victory over sin and its consequence, death.

The apostle Paul refers to Christ's absolute triumph over death in his letter to the church at Corinth:

Listen, I tell you a mystery: We will not all sleep, but we will all be changed—in a flash, in the twinkling of an eye, at the last trumpet. For the trumpet will sound, the dead will be raised imperishable, and we will be changed. For the perishable must clothe itself with the imperishable, and the mortal with immortality. When the perishable has been clothed with the imperishable, and the mortal with immortality, then the saying that is written will come true: "Death has been swallowed up in victory."

"Where, O death, is your victory?

Where, O death, is your sting?"

The sting of death is sin, and the power of sin is the law. But thanks be to God! He gives us the victory through our Lord Jesus Christ. (1 Corinthians 15:51-57)

After writing of the enslaving power of sin in Romans 7, Paul confessed to being helpless before it and, in verse 24, cried out in apparent despair: "What a wretched man I am! Who will rescue me from this body of death?" Immediately, he answered himself most definitively: "Thanks be to God— through Jesus Christ our Lord!" (v. 25). In the next four verses, he triumphantly describes the clear relationship between Christ's death and victory over sin:

Therefore, there is now no condemnation for those who are in Christ Jesus, because through Christ Jesus the law of the Spirit of life set me free from the law of sin and death. For what the law was powerless to do in that it was weakened by the sinful nature, God did by sending his own Son in the likeness of sinful man to be a sin offering. And so he condemned sin in sinful man, in order that the righteous requirements of the law might be fully met in us. (Romans 8:1-4a)

Gustaf Aulen, the twentieth-century Swedish Lutheran theologian, is perhaps most responsible for reintroducing this *Christus Victor* interpretation of the atonement to the holiness tradition. Commenting on the Patristic (early church fathers) understanding of the atonement, Aulen writes:

But in truth the classic idea of the Atonement, as it is set forth in the Fathers, is both clear and monumental. It sets forth God's coming to man, to accomplish His redemptive work; Incarnation and Redemption belong indissolubly together; God in Christ overcomes the hostile powers which hold man in bondage . . . The deliverance of man from the power of death and the devil is at the same time his deliverance from God's judgment. God is reconciled by His own act in reconciling the world to himself. Thus, the power of evil is broken.[5]

The importance of this interpretation of the atonement to a call to holiness is obvious. Christ can accomplish what humankind is helpless to do, no matter their resolve. The enslaving power of sin has been broken, and people inhabited by the Holy Spirit of Christ live with his power over sin.

This ancient understanding of Christ revealing God's power does not exhaust the biblical witness to the atonement, either. John Wesley held to the satisfaction theory formulated in the eleventh century by Anselm, archbishop of Canterbury. As Alister McGrath wrote in his *Christianity: An Introduction*, the "purpose of the incarnation was that God, through Christ, might be able to offer forgiveness, while at the same time satisfying and not offending against his own strict justice."[6] In short, Christ received humanity's deserved penalty for sin.

This is what I told that suffering young woman who had lived for years knowing that she deserved punishment for—to her, at least—what was the worst of all crimes. Yes, what she had done was wrong, and yes, punishment was in order, and yes, God's character of holy love demanded her punishment—but he received it in her place. And this is what the apostle Paul indicated was the reason for the cross, when he wrote:

> God presented [Christ] as a sacrifice of atonement, through faith in his blood. He did this to demonstrate his justice, because in his forbearance he had left the sins committed beforehand unpunished—he did it to demonstrate his justice at the present time, so as to be just and the one who justifies those who have faith in Jesus. (Romans 3:25-26)

In Romans 3:25 the NIV translates Paul's Greek as "sacrifice of atonement," but two English words are used more often: "propitiation" and "expiation." "Propitiation" refers to the wrath of God being satisfied, and "expiation" refers to the guilt of sin being cleansed. In their commentary on the book of Romans, William Greathouse and George Lyons reflect on expiation and propitiation:

> Although the more extreme understandings of both expiation and propitiation must be rejected, in reality, aspects of both are inherent in [the Greek word] and seem to some interpreters necessary to a balanced biblical doctrine.[7]

This "balanced biblical doctrine," which has been integral to the Christian faith, means that Jesus Christ received the punishment of a holy God for the sins of the world that was due the sinful creature. In this mysterious transaction, Christ became sin for sinful humanity; because of this act of obedient love on the part of the Savior, and because of his "passive righteousness," there is now freedom from the guilt and shame of sin for all who believe. In short, propitiation made expiation possible. As Wesley wrote:

> All believers are forgiven and accepted, not for the sake of anything in them, or of anything that ever was, that is, or ever can be done by them, but wholly and solely for the sake of what Christ hath done and suffered for them.[8]

Wesley so strongly believed in the meritorious sacrifice of Christ that he wrote, "The Christian Church stands or falls with it"[9] and, importantly, insisted that there would never be a time in the life of the believer when they would not need the atonement's saving work:

> And this is not only the means of our obtaining the favor of God, but of our continuing therein. It is thus we come to God at first; it is by the same we come unto him ever after. We walk in one and the same new and living way, till our spirit returns to God.[10]

This doctrine of atonement interpreted as propitiation and expiation is faithful to the Christian tradition as a whole. The Anglican bishop of Durham, N. T. Wright, affirms this in his book *The Crown and the Fire*:

> Jesus, the innocent one, was drawing on to himself the holy wrath of God against human sin in general, so that human sinners like you and me can find, as we look at the cross, that the load of sin and guilt we have been carrying is taken away from us. Jesus takes it on himself, and somehow absorbs it, so that when we look back there is nothing there.

Our sins have been dealt with and we need never carry their burden again.[11]

In the third chapter of Romans, and again in the eighth chapter, Paul wrote that God, through Christ, provided the sacrifice for sin that humanity could not: "For what the law was powerless to do in that it was weakened by the sinful nature, God did by sending his own Son *in the likeness of sinful man* to be a sin offering" (Romans 8:3, emphasis added). In other words, what humanity could never do, Christ did for us.

As might be expected, Paul wrote of this message of atonement to other churches as well. To the church of Corinth, he described the cross as transformative precisely because, on the cross, Christ generously assumed the sin of the world, accepted the judgment for that sin, and therefore made reconciliation between a holy God and sinful humankind possible:

> If anyone is in Christ, he is a new creation; the old has gone, the new has come! All this is from God, who reconciled us to himself through Christ and gave us the ministry of reconciliation: that God was reconciling the world to himself in Christ, *not counting men's sins against them . . .* God made him *who had no sin to be sin for us,* so that in him we might become the righteousness of God. (2 Corinthians 5:17-19*b,* 21, emphasis added)

Paul directly identified the cross as the place of God's judgment when he wrote to the churches of Galatia: "Christ redeemed us from the curse of the law *by becoming a curse for us,* for it is written: 'Cursed is everyone who is hung on a tree'" (Galatians 3:13, emphasis added).

This was not only Paul's interpretation. The apostle Peter also understood the cross as propitiation. He wrote that Christ "himself *bore our sins* in his body on the tree, so that we might die to sins and live for righteousness; by his wounds you have been healed" (1 Peter 2:24, emphasis added).

Peter, in the last phrase of that passage was simply quoting from Isaiah 53, written about seven hundred years before Christ's crucifixion. The prophet wrote:

> He was despised and rejected by men,
>> a man of sorrows, and familiar with suffering.

Like one from whom men hide their faces
>   he was despised, and we esteemed him not.
Surely *he took up our infirmities*
>   and carried our sorrows,
yet we considered him *stricken by God,*
>   smitten by him, and afflicted.
But he was pierced for our transgressions,
>   *he was crushed for our iniquities;*
the punishment that brought us peace was upon him,
>   *and by his wounds we are healed.*
We all, like sheep, have gone astray,
>   each of us has turned to his own way;
and *the* L*ORD* *has laid on him*
>   *the iniquity of us all.* (Isaiah 53:3-6, emphasis added)

The Gospels indicate that Jesus understood his death as satisfying God's wrath. All three Synoptic Gospels report that, in the garden on the night of his betrayal, Jesus prayed that God would release him from drinking the cup (Matthew 26:39). The Hebrews had a long tradition of likening God's judgment to drinking his "cup of wrath." Both Isaiah 51:17-22 and Jeremiah 25:15-28 refer to this "cup of wrath." John's vision in Revelation included that imagery—those who received the mark of the beast would "drink of the wine of God's fury, which has been poured full strength into the cup of his wrath" (Revelation 14:10). Thus, the most obvious interpretation of Jesus' earnest plea—"Father, if you are willing, take this cup from me" (Luke 22:42)—is that he was pleading for release from bearing the brunt of God's wrath and the subsequent separation from his Father. Jesus' cry from the cross, "My God, my God, why have you forsaken me?" (Mark 15:34), can be easily understood as the cry of one who was receiving the full force of God's judgment on sin.

N. T. Wright writes:

> On the cross [Jesus] took on himself that separation from God which all other men know. He did not deserve it; he had done nothing to warrant being cut off from God; but as he identified himself totally with sinful

humanity, the punishment which that sinful humanity deserved was laid fairly and squarely on his shoulders . . . That is why he shrank, in Gethsemane, from drinking the "cup" offered to him: he knew it to be the cup of God's wrath. On the cross, Jesus drank that cup to the dregs, so that his sinful people might not drink it. He drank it to the dregs. He finished it, finished the bitter cup both physically and spiritually . . . Here is the bill, and on it the word "finished"—"paid in full." The debt is paid. The punishment has been taken. Salvation is accomplished.[12]

In a commentary on Galatians 2, Martin Luther wrote: "Jesus Christ . . . upon the cross did bear in his body my sin . . . Christ was delivered for my sins, and was made accursed for me, that I might be delivered from everlasting death."[13]

In his sermon "Justification by Faith" Wesley wrote:

[The believer's] sins, all his past sins, in thought, word and deed, are covered, are blotted out, shall not be remembered or mentioned against him any more than if they had not been. God will not inflict on that sinner what he deserved to suffer because the Son of his love hath suffered for him. And from the time we are "accepted through the beloved," "reconciled to God through his blood," he loves and blesses and watches over us for good, even as if we had never sinned.[14]

Thus, the revelation of God through the cross of Christ is rich in meaning. The distinct aspects of atonement overlap one another; no one aspect is sufficient to comprehend what God has done for sinful humanity. The cross reveals God's victory over sin and death. It reveals the extravagant love of God and the sacrificial nature of his love. And it reveals that God himself was willing to receive the punishment that sinful humanity deserved. Thus, the cross reveals both God's judgment and mercy, which flow from his character of holy love. Indeed, without understanding the cross as God's judgment on sin, it is impossible to understand the full extent of his love. Furthermore, without understanding the cross as both judgment and mercy, as both wrath and love, it is impossible to appreciate the victory over sin—victory possible only because God receives the judgment that humankind deserves.

It was the cross that liberated that young woman from the self-loathing and condemnation that she knew she deserved. I witnessed how the atonement released her, a mother and wife, to live in humility and loving devotion to her God who had extravagantly forgiven her infinite sin. The relationship with her child and her husband was redeemed. And she no longer feared heaven, but eagerly awaited the coming kingdom when that redemption between her and her aborted child would be fully realized.

The cross as revealing God's love, justice, and intercession is wonderfully portrayed in Charles Wesley's hymn "Arise, My Soul, Arise." The beauty and power of this poetic word comes from its being grounded in a full understanding of the work of Christ as victor, as propitiator, as expiator—indeed, as love incarnate:

> Arise, my soul, arise,
>   shake off your guilty fears;
> The bleeding sacrifice,
>   in my behalf appears;
> Before the throne my Surety stands,
> Before the throne my Surety stands,
> My name is written on His hands.
>
> He ever lives above,
>   for me to intercede;
> His all redeeming love,
>   His precious blood, to plead;
> His blood atoned for all our race,
> His blood atoned for all our race,
> And sprinkles now the throne of grace.
>
> Five bleeding wounds He bears;
>   received on Calvary;
> They pour effectual prayers;
>   they strongly plead for me:
> "Forgive him, O forgive," they cry,
> "Forgive him, O forgive," they cry,
> "Nor let that ransomed sinner die!"

The Father hears Him pray,
    His dear anointed One;
He cannot turn away
    the presence of His Son;
The Spirit answers to the blood,
The Spirit answers to the blood
And tells me I am born of God.

My God is reconciled;
    His pardoning voice I hear;
He owns me for His child;
    I can no longer fear.
With confidence I now draw nigh,
With confidence I now draw nigh,
And "Father, Abba, Father," cry.[15]

God has reconciled himself to the world through the death of his Son, which made it possible for the world to be reconciled to him. Liberation from the guilt and power of sin is now possible because of this unilateral, gracious sacrifice of Christ on the cross. The Lord is our righteousness. And the apostle Paul's rhetorical question in Romans 3:27, "Where, then, is boasting?" is forever answered, "It is excluded."

FAITH

6
JUSTIFICATION BY FAITH

"Though I lived as a monk without reproach, I felt that I was a sinner before God
with an extremely disturbed conscience. I could not believe that He was placated
by my satisfaction . . . At last, by the mercy of God, meditating day and night,
I gave heed to the context of the words, namely . . . 'He who through faith is
righteous shall live.' There I began to understand that the righteousness of God
is that by which the righteous lives by a gift of God, namely by faith . . .
Here I felt that I was altogether born again and had entered
paradise itself through open gates" (Martin Luther).[1]

◆

So here's the good news stated simply: salvation is pure gift. The reconciliation that takes place between a holy God and sinful humanity is a reconciliation that God has made possible. God initiated the reconciliation, and God is the one who preserves it. Forgiveness for sin is not deserved, and continued liberation from sin is not a work. God himself provides the righteousness that characterizes this restored relationship. And the only contingency upon which this righteousness depends is acceptance of this as an undeserved gift. The good news stated as simply as possible is this: salvation is a free gift from God and is available to all those who would simply believe it. Justification is by faith. In other words, being made righteous is a result of trusting in the faithfulness of Christ to make us righteous. That's the gospel.

But "justification by faith" is one of the most difficult claims to believe in all of Christianity. If the apostle Paul's letters are any indication, not only is it difficult to believe initially, but also it is the promise most quickly forsaken, even among those who have experienced its reality, and it is the easiest from which to deviate. In my limited experience, its unapologetic proclamation is rare. And when the promise of salvation as pure gift is proclaimed, it is often followed by careful qualifications so that its claim might not be presumed on. When John Wesley was preaching all over England, it wasn't his holiness preaching that led to his being forbidden to preach in those same pulpits, but his bold preaching of justification by faith. In his journal, he wrote:

> Sunday, May 14, 1738 — I preached in the morning at St. Ann's, Aldersgate; and in the afternoon at the Savoy Chapel, free salvation by faith in the blood of Christ. I was quickly apprised that at St. Ann's, likewise, I am to preach no more.[2]

And yet, this audacious promise of salvation as pure gift is at the heart of the Christian faith, and it would not be too strong to say that any dilution of this promise risks the very possibility of that salvation. (See the book of Galatians for evidence of this.)

This Protestant proclamation declares that people are made righteous by trusting in Christ's faithfulness for that righteousness. That is the beginning of salvation, but it also must be understood that is the middle as well as the end of salvation. It is never *not* true for the believer. We are made righteous (justified) by trusting in Christ to make us righteous on the first day of salvation, as well as on the last. Martin Luther's reemphasis of this "Protestant principle" liberated him from the slavery of trying to be holy for salvation's sake, which turmoil many in the holiness tradition understand. And two weeks after Wesley preached its promise at St. Ann's, he himself experienced the liberation that comes from such faith. In what has likely become the single most often used quote of all of John Wesley's writings, he testified to the change that came to him:

> In the evening I went very unwillingly to a society in Aldersgate Street, where one was reading Luther's preface to the Epistle to the Romans. About a quarter before nine, while the leader was describing the change which God works in the heart through faith in Christ, I felt my heart strangely warmed. I felt I did trust in Christ alone for salvation; and an assurance was given me that He had taken away my sins, even mine, and saved me from the law of sin and death.[3]

Trusting in Christ for salvation is the way of salvation. That is the good news. That is the gospel.

In Romans 3:21-26, the apostle Paul described how it was that sinful humanity received this grace of salvation:

This righteousness from God comes through faith in Jesus Christ to all who believe. There is no difference, for all have sinned and fall short of the glory of God, and are justified freely by his grace through the redemption that came by Christ Jesus. (Romans 3:22-24)

The apostle Paul then illustrated this promise by using one of the most significant people in the history of the Jewish faith tradition. He explained that Abraham became the father of the Jewish faith, not because of any personal or achieved righteousness, but because he simply believed! Paul's powerful words, in which he described Abraham's unwavering faith, are intended to describe every Christian's faith:

Against all hope, Abraham in hope believed and so became the father of many nations . . . he did not waver through unbelief regarding the promise of God, but was strengthened in his faith and gave glory to God, being fully persuaded that God had power to do what he had promised. This is why "it was credited to him as righteousness." The words "it was credited to him" were written not for him alone, but also for us, to whom God will credit righteousness—for us who believe in him who raised Jesus our Lord from the dead. (Romans 4:18, 20-24)

Every Christian's confidence is not in his or her own ability to fulfill God's expectations. On the contrary, Christians are those who are made acutely aware of their inability to fulfill any of God's expectations. And yet, this doesn't cause despair, for their confidence is not in their own strength, but in God who fulfills his promises. Christians are those who acknowledge their helplessness to fulfill God's commands, and yet continue to believe that God himself can still fulfill them. Salvation is a pure act of grace, a free gift from God whom we are trusting for that salvation.

William Greathouse and George Lyons wrote of the absolute character of this faith in their commentary on Romans 4:

Faith is not a refined kind of righteousness that God accepts instead of legal obedience . . . Faith is not relying on human trust; it is relying on God. Believing is not something people do instead of obeying the

Law as a means of winning God's approval. The point Paul makes is that faith is not a work, not something people do at all . . . People are not justified by the virtue of their faith, but by God . . . Faith trusts in God's word and work so completely that it despairs of human work as a means of gaining God's favor. In a sense, faith is nothing more than grateful receptivity to God's gift.[4]

Being made righteous as an absolute gift of grace was not a minor theme in Paul's writings. Almost every letter attributed to Paul articulates this fundamental claim. To the churches of Ephesus, Paul wrote: "It is by grace you have been saved, through faith—and this not from yourselves, it is the gift of God" (Ephesians 2:8). And he told the church at Philippi that he considered as manure any good he might have claimed for his glory! He didn't want any righteousness other than the righteousness that came from God and was by faith (Philippians 3:4b-9).

This way of salvation is affirmed in the great faith traditions of the Protestant churches. The United Methodist Article of Faith on justification is virtually identical with the Anglican Article:

Article IX: Of the Justification of Man

We are accounted righteous before God only for the merit of our Lord and Savior Jesus Christ, by faith, and not for our own works or deservings. Wherefore, that we are justified by faith, only, is a most wholesome doctrine, and very full of comfort.[5]

One might expect that the Lutheran tradition would strongly affirm the same. The Augsburg Confession, to which the Lutheran traditions still adhere, is clear:

Article IV: Of Justification.

1] Also they teach that men cannot be justified before God by their own strength, merits, or works, but are freely justified for 2] Christ's sake, through faith, when they believe that they are received into favor, and that their sins are forgiven for Christ's sake, who, by His death, has made satisfaction for our sins. 3] This faith God imputes for righteousness in His sight.[6]

The Church of the Nazarene's article, which combines statements on justification, regeneration, and adoption, recognizes this as well:

Article IX

9. We believe that justification is the gracious and judicial act of God by which He grants full pardon of all guilt and complete release from the penalty of sins committed, and acceptance as righteous, to all who believe on Jesus Christ and receive Him as Lord and Savior. . . .

12. We believe that justification, regeneration, and adoption are simultaneous in the experience of seekers after God and are obtained upon the condition of faith.[7]

Greathouse and Lyons summarize this evangelical promise this way: "To be justified by grace through faith is to be given a righteousness that one does not deserve."[8] Salvation is all gift.

Again, this gospel message is initially difficult to believe, and it may be even more difficult to keep believing. Even among those who have experienced the reality of initial salvation received as pure gift, the recurring temptation is to believe that continued salvation depends on some kind of works-righteousness. Believers are tempted to think that continued salvation depends on a person's ability to obey the law. This has been a particular issue for those in the holiness tradition who believe holiness is a present imperative and an earthly possibility. A popular understanding of the way of salvation among people in the holiness tradition is that initial salvation is certainly a free gift of grace but that holiness was subsequently an achievement. God certainly saves, but it's up to the believer to sanctify! Salvation was a gift, but holiness had to be earned! While it was never an official statement, this way of thinking resulted in a folk theology that insisted that justification, or reconciliation with God, was contingent on holiness, which was a person's responsibility. Salvation therefore was made identical to some sort of achieved holiness. The effect of this popular understanding was that the gospel proclamation of justification by faith was completely undermined.

The promise and power of the Wesleyan-holiness message, however, is not in proclaiming the possibility of a realized holiness. It is found in proclaiming that sanctification, which is the work of God making us holy and which begins at justification, is received by faith. Holiness is God's gift of grace every bit as much as our forgiveness from sins! People are not only justified (declared righteous) by grace through faith but also sanctified (made holy) by God's grace through faith. Salvation—from beginning to end and all through the middle—is a gift.

All Christian faith traditions assert that God not only declares sinful humanity righteous at the moment of justification but also begins to make sinful humanity righteous. Sanctification begins with justification. Not only is the relationship between God and man restored, but God begins the actual transformation process. This is what the apostle Paul promised the people of Rome when he wrote, "But now that you have been set free from sin and have become slaves to God, the benefit you reap leads to holiness, and the result is eternal life" (Romans 6:22). This is what he promised the people of Corinth when he wrote, "Therefore, if anyone is in Christ, he is a new creation; the old has gone, the new has come!" (2 Corinthians 5:17). This is what he promised the Ephesians when he wrote that they were "created to be like God in true righteousness and holiness" (Ephesians 4:24b).

The process of being made holy begins at the moment of justification. This means that sinful humanity is not only justified by faith but also sanctified by faith. Sanctification is no more earned than salvation. In this, John Wesley was clear. In his message "The Scripture Way of Salvation" he gives a comprehensive explanation of the way of salvation:

> I have continually testified in private and in public, that we are sanctified as well as justified by faith. And indeed the one of those great truths does exceedingly illustrate the other. Exactly as we are justified by faith, so are we sanctified by faith. Faith is the condition, and the only condition, of sanctification, exactly as it is of justification. It is the condition: none is sanctified but he that believes; without faith no man is sanctified. And it is the only condition: this alone is sufficient for sanctification. Every one that believes is sanctified, whatever else he has or has not. In other words, no man is sanctified till he believes: every man when he believes is sanctified.[9]

Wesleyan scholar Kenneth J. Collins commented on Wesley's confidence that sanctification as well as justification was by grace through faith:

> Wesley's breakthrough . . . had to do with his surprising realization that the holiness that had so captivated his imagination . . . would be actualized in this life, neither by works, nor by resolve, nor by human will and effort, however well motivated or sincere, but simply and wonderfully as a result of divine graciousness and favor.[10]

This priority of faith in sanctification is indicated in "Of Sanctification," from the Articles of Religion of the United Methodist Church, and illustrates thorough consistency with John Wesley's understanding:

> Sanctification is that renewal of our fallen nature by the Holy Ghost, received through faith in Jesus Christ, whose blood of atonement cleanses from all sin; whereby we are not only delivered from the guilt of sin, but are washed from its pollution, saved from its power, and are enabled, through grace, to love God with all our hearts and to walk in his holy commandments blameless.[11]

"Entire Sanctification," from the Article of Faith for the Church of the Nazarene, specifically describes the aspect of sanctification that indicates the priority of faith.

> Entire sanctification is provided by the blood of Jesus, is wrought instantaneously *by faith*, preceded by entire consecration; and to this work and state of grace the Holy Spirit bears witness.[12]

The Protestant principle *sola fide,* or "faith alone," is true for those seeking to be justified and is true for those seeking to be sanctified. The testimony of the Bible and the testimony of the tradition is clear. Salvation from beginning to end is solely contingent on trusting in Christ for that full salvation. Sinful humanity is justified and sanctified by faith.

To illustrate the absolute inadequacy of anything other than "grace through faith" to provide salvation, and in an effort to reveal the foolishness of claiming any kind of personally achieved holiness, I have asked those who find this gospel difficult to believe to imagine themselves before God on judgment day. I ask them to imagine themselves before that great white throne, before which the book of Revelation promises we all will stand. I

then follow up that suggestion with several questions, which are all variations of the same one. I ask, "Before that throne of judgment, what will
you plead?" "How will you justify yourself before God's awe-inspiring, fear-
provoking holiness?" "What will you say before the holiness of God?" And I
then suggest answers they might want to offer God. "Will you recount your
faithful attendance to Sunday school or church?" "Will you remind God
of your weekly tithe and your extra giving to missions periodically?" "Will
you argue your being a better than average human being?" "Would you
even point to your martyrdom, should you ever have the privilege of being
martyred?" To reveal the absolute inadequacy of ever being able to justify
oneself by claiming any achievements, I ask, "Before the awful holiness of
God, what will you dare to plead?"

Those who take the exercise seriously acknowledge that no self-justification will be sufficient on that day, no matter how devoted or sacrificial
they were in life. Those who take the exercise seriously recognize that the
only justification sufficient before the holiness of God will be the justification
that comes by trusting in Jesus Christ. Those who take the exercise seriously
know that the only plea sufficient on that day will be the blood of Jesus
Christ. And they will plead the blood.

The apostle Paul recognized this in his letter to the church at Philippi:

But whatever was to my profit I now consider loss for the sake of Christ.
What is more, I consider everything a loss compared to the surpassing
greatness of knowing Christ Jesus my Lord, for whose sake I have lost
all things. I consider them rubbish, that I may gain Christ and be found
in him, not having a righteousness of my own that comes from the law,
but that which is through faith in Christ—the righteousness that comes
from God and is by faith. (Philippians 3:7-9)

And this is what Charlotte Elliot understood when she penned "Just As
I Am" in 1835:

Just as I am, without one plea,
But that Thy blood was shed for me,
And that Thou bidst me come to Thee,
O Lamb of God, I come, I come.

Just as I am, poor, wretched, blind;
Sight, riches, healing of the mind,
Yea, all I need in Thee to find,
O Lamb of God, I come, I come.

Just as I am, Thou wilt receive,
Wilt welcome, pardon, cleanse, relieve;
Because Thy promise I believe,
O Lamb of God, I come, I come.[13]

Justification and sanctification by grace through faith means that this hymn is true for believers, no matter how long they have believed. Justification is by trusting in Christ for salvation, or there is no justification at all. Sanctification is by trusting in Christ for that holiness or there is no sanctification at all. It is grace upon grace. This is the truth of the gospel.

I was several years into ministry before I truly understood this primary claim of the gospel and I remember very clearly my "Aldersgate." I had been writing Bible studies from the book of Romans for the small-group ministry at my church and was immersed in commentaries; evidently, this prolonged reflection and serious meditation on Romans was an effective means of grace. One morning in prayer, I was reminded of all of the commitments I had made to God through the years. I had released my future plans by following God's call to the ministry. I had sought God's permission in marrying my wife. Moving to Illinois to pastor was a consequence of discerning God's will for us at that point. I had surrendered my children to him when they were young. In short, my life, though not uniquely so, has been characterized by repeated commitments to discerning, and then obeying, God's will. That morning in prayer, as God brought these past consecrations to mind, he asked me to make at least one more. He asked for a commitment that I had never considered and hadn't even known was possible. He asked me to give my salvation to him. I wasn't sure what that meant, and it took some time to process the implications of that consecration. As I reflected on the nature of this commitment, I began to understand that God was asking to let him save me, and to quit trying to save myself. He was asking me to trust him with my salvation, instead of trusting in myself. He was asking me to allow him to be my justification and sanctification, to stop trying to justify and sanctify my-self, and was asking me to allow him to be Lord, even of my salvation. That morning in prayer, he asked for a commitment I didn't even know I needed to make: *Why don't you give me your salvation?*

I gave it to him and recognized that my previous confidence had been in my ability to obey, and not in the God who would save and sanctify me. At some level, I had been trying to earn my salvation through my repeated consecrations and obedience. I had not been living conscious of the com-prehensive and overwhelming nature of God's grace. As a result, I hadn't been living out the ethic of holiness in gratitude for salvation already re-ceived. I had been trying to keep God's grace by working for it. That morn-ing, I began to understand the nature of salvation as a pure gift and faith as the simple response of trusting in Christ for that gift. I began to understand that salvation is all grace through faith. It is grace upon grace. While I can't confess that "my heart was strangely warmed" as John Wesley's heart was, I can confess that I was given a peace and assurance I hadn't known prior to that particular consecration, which is with me still. This I know more than anything else: God is saving me. God is sanctifying me. He is working in me, working out my salvation.

Consequently, promises that had been difficult to believe prior to that morning became real. Paul's promise to the Philippians of assurance of final salvation became true for me:

> In all my prayers for all of you, I always pray with joy because of your partnership in the gospel from the first day until now, being confident of this, that he who began a good work in you will carry it on to com-pletion until the day of Christ Jesus. (Philippians 1:4-6)

Paul's testimony to Timothy of assurance of final salvation became true for me:

> Yet I am not ashamed, because I know whom I have believed, and am convinced that he is able to guard what I have entrusted to him for that day. (2 Timothy 1:12*b*)

Paul's promise to the church at Rome of the result of such trust in Christ's salvation became true for me:

Therefore, since we have been justified through faith, we have peace with God through our Lord Jesus Christ, through whom we have gained access by faith into this grace in which we now stand. And we rejoice in the hope of the glory of God. Not only so, but we also rejoice in our sufferings, because we know that suffering produces perseverance; perseverance, character; and character, hope. And hope does not disappoint us, because God has poured out his love into our hearts by the Holy Spirit, whom he has given us. . . .

Since we have now been justified by his blood, how much more shall we be saved from God's wrath through him! For if, when we were God's enemies, we were reconciled to him through the death of his Son, how much more, having been reconciled, shall we be saved through his life! Not only is this so, but we also rejoice in God through our Lord Jesus Christ, through whom we have now received reconciliation. (Romans 5:1-5, 9-11)

Trusting in Christ for salvation is the way of salvation, from beginning to end. That is the good news. That is the gospel.

The significance of this Christian truth to a doctrine of holiness is clear. Recognizing the author of our salvation, and from whom our salvation comes, undermines any and all pride for righteousness achieved; pride is the antithesis of holiness. If it is all grace, then salvation is always undeserved and the only response possible is humility and grateful love. If salvation is not all grace, then holiness pursued in gratitude can easily become prideful legalism—self-justifying and enslaving. As John Wesley wrote:

One reason, however, we may humbly conceive, of God's fixing this condition of justification — "If thou believest in the Lord Jesus Christ thou shalt be saved" — was to hide pride from man . . . And such is faith. It is peculiarly fitted for this end. For he that cometh unto God by this faith must fix his eye singly on his own wickedness, on his guilt and helplessness, without having the least regard to any supposed good in himself, to any virtue or righteousness whatsoever. He must come to God as a *mere sinner* . . . Thus only can he be "found in him" and receive the "righteousness which is of God by faith."[14]

Thus, a revitalized call to holiness requires recognizing the relational character of a holy God who hates sin for love's sake. It requires recognizing that humanity is enslaved to sin and unable to save itself. It demands we recognize that salvation has been provided through the atoning blood of Jesus Christ, and that salvation, from beginning to end, is all grace. It is from grace to grace. And ultimately, it requires that we recognize this truth: we are made righteous by trusting in Christ for that righteousness.

7

THE LAW ESTABLISHED
THROUGH FAITH

"In the New Testament, religion is grace and ethics is gratitude"
(Thomas Erskine).[1]

═══════════════════ ◆ ═══════════════════

When I was in high school, we were required to pass a U.S. Constitution test. All seniors were required to take this test, which was given over two days at several different times. It just so happened that one of my friends got a copy of the test from another student and offered it to me as a "study guide." The pressure to pass a test without studying for it proved too great a temptation and I memorized the answers, passing the test with relative ease.

It wasn't long before the Holy Spirit began to faithfully convict me for cheating, and I was forced to deal with a very guilty conscience. However, I was unsure of the penalty for having cheated on this test; I didn't want to risk any penalty, so I began to search out a solution for my guilt that would not require a confession of cheating. I found the answer in my own distorted theory of atonement. I reasoned that, since I was a sinner and since Christ had died for my sins, he had taken the punishment and penalty that I deserved. I don't think I knew the name of the substitutionary theory of the atonement—which I was, in fact, inappropriately using effectively—but I reasoned that since Jesus had died on the cross, I shouldn't have to atone for my own sins; that his "substitution" meant I would not have to suffer the penalty of having cheated on that particular test. I skillfully reasoned that Christ's blood covered that sin, which ultimately meant I was free to reap the benefit of cheating. And I was so proud of my astute theologizing that I even bragged to several of my friends about this liberty to sin that Christ's death afforded me. As an aside, they did not seem nearly as impressed with my theology as I was.

I really wish I could write that I came to my senses, confessed my sin, and accepted the punishment. But I didn't do that. As a matter of fact, I had rationalized my cheating so well that I didn't think about that incident much since then. I wish I had had a greater appreciation for what Christ did on the cross; instead, I have a personal illustration of the mercenary use of Christ's death to justify sin.

This idea that Christ's death exempts believers from the moral law is called antinomianism—literally translated, "lawlessness." Antinomianism says that since obedience to the law cannot make one righteous, and since righteousness is a pure gift of God's grace, then those justified are allowed to ignore the moral law. My embracing such an antinomian understanding of the gospel was an obvious, self-justifying perversion of the faith; however, this happens all the time, as is captured nicely in the common quip, "Better to ask for forgiveness than permission." If the book of Romans is any indication, making allowance for sin by presuming on God's grace is as old as the gospel itself. This idea that justification by faith allows for continuing in sin without penalty was evidently threatening the integrity of the gospel in Rome; immediately following the apostle Paul's declaration of what God did for humanity through Christ Jesus, and of how this pure gift of salvation was received by faith, Paul was forced to strongly repudiate this antinomian understanding of grace. He did so with the pointed rhetorical question: "What shall we say, then? Shall we go on sinning that grace may increase?" (6:1). His forceful answer, the strength of which is difficult to translate from the Greek, was a definitive "No" (v. 2). Attempts at translating the Greek include "God forbid" (KJV); "By no means!" (NIV); "Certainly not!" (AB); "May it never be!" (NASB). To Paul, the idea that one justified by grace through faith would continue to live a life of sin was inconceivable.

It was also inconceivable to John Wesley, and this is why he was so critical of certain aspects of the Calvinism of his day. While Wesley agreed with the Reformed doctrines of total depravity and justification by faith, he decisively parted company with them in the doctrines of unconditional election, limited atonement, irresistible grace, and the perseverance of saints—summarized by the acronym "TULIP"—precisely because he felt that these led to an indifference to holiness. When Wesley was asked to distinguish his understanding of salvation from the Calvinist, he made it very clear that it was not in reference to either *total depravity* (T in TULIP) or justification by faith. In several of these clarifications, he used one of his favorite expressions—"hair's breadth"—to describe how close he and Calvin were in those particular doctrines. In a conversation in August of 1745, Wesley reported:

Q. 22. Does not the truth of the gospel lie very near both to Calvinism and Antinomianism?

A. Indeed it does; as it were, within a hair's breadth . . .

Q. 23. Wherein may we come to the very edge of Calvinism?

A. (1.) In ascribing all good to the free grace of God. (2.) In denying all natural free will, and all power antecedent to grace. And, (3.) In excluding all merit from man; even for what he has or does by the grace of God.[2]

As late as 1765, in a letter to a friend, Wesley succinctly declared his harmony with Calvin on justification through faith: "I think on Justification just as I have done any time these seven-and-twenty years; and just as Mr. Calvin does. In this respect I do not differ from him an hair's breadth."[3]

The necessity of such a "reformed" understanding of justification to a doctrine of holiness has already been described. As was noted in the previous chapter, Wesley once wrote: "One reason, however, we may humbly conceive, of God's fixing this condition of justification — 'If thou believest in the Lord Jesus Christ thou shalt be saved' — was to hide pride from man."[4]

The Reformed doctrines with which Wesley disagreed, and vehemently, are those of the last four letters of TULIP: Unconditional election (God alone chooses those who will be saved), Limited atonement (Christ did not die for all, but only for the elect), Irresistible grace (a person cannot prevent his or her salvation), and Perseverance of the saints (once saved, always saved). According to Wesley, these doctrines powerfully undercut all personal responsibility for salvation, undermined any incentive to holiness, and in his mind, led inevitably to antinomianism.

In short, if God's sovereign decree was such that the elect were unconditionally predestined to salvation, were irresistibly saved, and would persevere in that salvation regardless of the will of those so elected, then the call to holiness was superfluous. According to Wesley, Calvin's full doctrine did nothing less than "stab Christ in the house of his friends." Wesley wrote:

> For wherever this doctrine is cordially received, it leaves no place for holiness. It demolishes it from top to bottom; it destroys both root and branch. It effectually tears up all desire of it, all endeavor after it. It forbids all such exhortations as might excite those desires, or awaken those endeavors. Nay, it makes men afraid of personal holiness, afraid of cherishing any thought of it, or motion toward it, lest they should deny the faith, and reject Christ and his righteousness: So that, instead of being "zealous of good works," they are a stink in their nostrils.[5]

That Calvinism led inevitably to antinomianism in Wesley's mind can be seen in his linking the two in the question quoted earlier: "Does not the truth of the gospel lie very near both to Calvinism and Antinomianism?" According to the Wesleyan-holiness tradition, God's grace gives no license to sin, no matter how deeply rooted the sin's nature or comprehensive the grace of God.

Those in the holiness tradition, under the tutelage of Wesley and his theological heirs, have been keenly aware of the dangers of antinomianism to the message of holiness. The call to holiness is, by definition, an explicit rejection of the idea that Christians continue to sin after justification. This fear of a "sinning Christianity," however, led the holiness movement to an equally dangerous perversion of the gospel: legalism.

The charge of legalism, understood across all theological traditions, refers to the notion that justification depends on obedience to the moral law of God. Some Christians' faith, undeniably, devolves into a "works-righteousness," but this would not be unique to the holiness tradition. If Paul's letter to the churches of Galatia is any indication, the idea that salvation must be maintained through obedience to the law is as old as the church itself.

The charge of legalism with which the holiness movement in particular has had to contend is related to the idea that holiness depends on obedience to the moral law. Some in the holiness movement understood initial salvation as God's gift of grace, but then believed that progress to holiness was a human achievement. Wesley rejected this, but the temptation to works-righteousness for the sake of holiness is a common misunderstanding of the holiness message.

This inclination to a legalistic understanding of the nature of holiness is illustrated by the special rules that many holiness denominations adopted as indicative of a holy life. The effort to prescribe "holiness" resulted in the adoption of very specific prohibitions of behaviors considered inconsistent with a holy ethic. Such prohibitions included drinking or selling alcohol, attending the theater, swimming with the opposite gender, shopping on Sundays, gambling, and smoking or chewing tobacco. The charge of legalism is often directed toward those specific rules. Implicit in this criticism is the legitimate complaint that holiness, while prohibiting particular behaviors, should not be comprehensively defined simply by the avoidance of such behaviors.

Understanding the call to holiness primarily as the successful performance of particular behaviors is the testimony of many in the holiness movement. This legalistic misunderstanding of holiness was truly harmful to the faith of many. The sad irony is that this legalistic interpretation of salvation was adamantly rejected by the apostle Paul in his letter to the Galatians two millennia ago and rejected by Wesley two centuries ago. Holiness is by grace through faith, and any legalistic interpretation of a doctrine of holiness is not gospel.

Today, this healthy opposition to legalism is resulting in the opposite error. The popular arguments heard today against a legalistic understanding of holiness are very similar to those that Paul fought against in the book of Romans. A modern take on one ancient contention is that since we are saved by grace through faith, we need not attend to the law at all. Obedience to the law as indicating one's attitude toward and relationship with God is dismissed as legalism. Indeed, the idea that the law might have continued authority over the Christian merely indicates that one has yet to understand the freedom from the law inherent in the gospel message itself.

This contemporary, superficial understanding of "liberation from legalism" is resulting in a toleration of sin and a casual indifference to the pursuit of holiness, which were precisely John Wesley's concerns. While no one would testify out loud to this (mis)understanding of the gospel, the similarities in behaviors and attitudes between believers and nonbelievers indicate that "liberation from legalism" has underlying, destructive deficiencies that need to be recognized. It is precisely this indifference to pursuing holiness on the part of those so "justified" that has led some, sadly, to undermine justification by faith alone—and, in a pernicious twist, to legitimize the defining of righteousness in terms of legalism!

Fear of legalistic Christianity is resulting in an embrace of the opposing, yet equally destructive, error of antinomianism, which denies the necessity of a law at all. Though the fear of antinomianism led to legalism, the current rejection of "legalism," popularly understood, is leading to an antinomianism every bit as destructive to the life of holiness as was the rejection of antinomianism that led to legalism.

These corresponding errors—both destructive to the pursuit of holiness—are not new and are driven in part by an inadequate understanding of the nature of justification. Indeed, these twin threats can only be navigated safely if we understand the truly transformative work of God as a consequence of justification by faith.

The idea that justification by faith meant that one could continue in sin was reprehensible to the apostle Paul. His adamant "No!" in response to the question "What shall we say, then? Shall we go on sinning so that grace may increase?" should give us no doubt. He continued:

> Or don't you know that all of us who were baptized into Christ Jesus were baptized into his death? We were therefore buried with him through baptism into death in order that, just as Christ was raised from the dead through the glory of the Father, we too may live a new life. If we have been united with him like this in his death, we will certainly also be united with him in his resurrection. For we know that our old self was crucified with him so that the body of sin might be done away with, that we should no longer be slaves to sin—because anyone who has died has been freed from sin. (Romans 6:1, 3-7)

According to the apostle Paul in Romans 6, when we are justified by faith, our entire orientation, our entire world, is changed. We step into a new reality, with Christ as Savior and King, which results in a new way of being.

Justification by faith through grace is transformative. It is regenerative. To combine the language of the apostles John and Paul, it is nothing less than being born again as a new creation. In language very familiar to the Wesleyan-holiness tradition, when we begin trusting in the justifying grace of God, sanctification begins! At justification, we are made righteous and we begin being made righteous. This was Wesley's understanding. In Wesley's sermon "The Scripture Way of Salvation," which Wesley scholar Albert Outler calls one of the most successful summaries of the Wesleyan way of salvation, he wrote:

> At the same time that we are justified, yea, in that very moment, sanctification begins. In that instant we are "born again," "born from above," "born of the Spirit." There is a *real* as well as a *relative* change. We are inwardly renewed by the power of God.[6]

In light of the transformative nature of justifying grace, it is easy to understand why the apostle Paul found it inconceivable that Christians would continue in sin after justification. Greathouse and Lyons go so far as to say:

> Christians *cannot* continue their former careers as sinners . . . Because of what Christ has done for us, we are no longer helpless slaves to sin. In fact, the enslaving power of sin in our lives is broken. Sin no longer reigns as master. Through the liberating power of Christ's saving death, we are free not to sin. For the first time in our lives we can say no to sin.[7]

To understand the absurdity of continuing in sin after justification, it might be helpful to imagine the apostle Paul asking the rhetorical question of Romans 6:1: "What shall we say, then? Shall we go on sinning?" It is inconceivable, in light of what God had done for him, that Paul would ever consider reentering the life from which God rescued him. It would be as if he were to ask God if he could continue his life of hatred and murderous behavior now that he had been made a new creation. In the words of Paul: *"We died to sin; how can we live in it any longer?"* (Romans 6:2, emphasis added).

Paul believed that justification, which initiates the sanctifying process, would reorient one's life so that holiness, or Christlikeness, would result. In Romans 6, Paul wrote of liberation from sin and he also wrote, "But now that you have been set free from sin and have become slaves to God, the benefit you reap *leads to holiness,* and the result is eternal life" (Romans 6:22, emphasis added). The life of one justified by grace should progress to a fully realized holiness, the process of which begins at the moment of justification. The result of God's gracious work in the lives of those justified and initially sanctified actually leads to the fulfillment of the moral law, not indifference to it! In a remarkable passage, the apostle Paul declared that Jesus Christ "condemned sin in sinful man, in order that *the righteous requirements of the law might be fully met in us,* who do not live according to the sinful nature but according to the Spirit" (Romans 8:3*b*-4, emphasis added). In other words, at justification, which is the beginning of sanctification, the moral law ceases to be a an extrinsic constraint and becomes an expression of the intrinsic life of God in the believer. Borrowing the words of the prophet Jeremiah, the law of God would no longer be written on tablets of stone, which invite breaking, but written on the flesh of the recreated heart, which delights in their fulfillment. In short, the law of God becomes embodied within the believer. When the law is understood in this way—as an imparted gift—then the words of the psalmist become appropriate for the justified: "His delight is in the law of the LORD, and on his law he meditates day and night" (Psalm 1:2).

Thus legalism, understood as earning righteousness, is precluded. Fulfilling the law is only possible through being made righteous by grace through the faith that confesses the absolute inability to become righteous apart from that empowering grace of God. The justified and initially sanctified believer need not work for righteousness, because righteousness has been given as a gift as a consequence of the restored relationship!

Thus antinomianism, understood as acquiescence to sin after justification, is excluded. By virtue of God's justification, the believer is freed from the power of sin, and fulfilling the law is a consequence of this incredible gift of righteousness by grace through faith. In other words, the call to holiness can only be understood in a way that is not destructively legalistic or dismissed as an impossibility by understanding the transforming power of justification.

This understanding of justification is what compelled the apostle Paul to call on followers of Christ to live without sin. In every letter he wrote, Paul called the churches to holiness. After writing of how justification by faith afforded freedom from sin's slavery, Paul instructed them to live without sin, which Christ's death had now made possible. A few examples from Paul's letters should be sufficient to indicate his expectation for those who had been so undeservedly justified. To the church at Thessalonica, he wrote:

> May he strengthen your hearts so that you will be blameless and holy in the presence of our God and Father when our Lord Jesus comes with all his holy ones. Finally, brothers, we instructed you how to live in order to please God, as in fact you are living. Now we ask you and urge you in the Lord Jesus to do this more and more. For you know what instructions we gave you by the authority of the Lord Jesus. It is God's will that you should be sanctified. (1 Thessalonians 3:13—4:3a)

A few paragraphs later, he reiterated the expectation:

> Be joyful always; pray continually; give thanks in all circumstances, for this is God's will for you in Christ Jesus. Do not put out the Spirit's fire; do not treat prophecies with contempt. Test everything. Hold on to the good. Avoid every kind of evil. May God himself, the God of peace, sanctify you through and through. May your whole spirit, soul and body be kept blameless at the coming of our Lord Jesus Christ. The one who calls you is faithful and he will do it. (5:16-24)

To the churches of Rome, he wrote:

> Therefore, I urge you, brothers, in view of God's mercy, to offer your bodies as living sacrifices, holy and pleasing to God—this is your spiritual act of worship. Do not conform any longer to the pattern of this world, but be transformed by the renewing of your mind. Then you will be able to test and approve what God's will is—his good, pleasing and perfect will. (Romans 12:1-2)

To the church at Corinth, he wrote:

> Since we have these promises, dear friends, let us purify ourselves from everything that contaminates body and spirit, perfecting holiness out of reverence for God. (2 Corinthians 7:1)

To the church at Ephesus, he wrote:

> You were taught, with regard to your former way of life, to put off your old self, which is being corrupted by its deceitful desires; to be made new in the attitude of your minds; and to put on the new self, created to be like God in true righteousness and holiness. (Ephesians 4:22-24)

This illustrates that the call to holiness is anything but legalistic or impossible when we correctly understand the transforming, sanctifying power of justification. According to Wesley,

> We allow that the state of a justified person is inexpressibly great and glorious. He is born again . . . He is a child of God, a member of Christ, an heir of the kingdom of heaven . . . His very body is the temple of the Holy Ghost . . . He is created anew in Christ Jesus. He is washed, he is *sanctified.* His heart is purified by faith; he is cleansed from the corruption that is in the world; the love of God is shed abroad in his heart by the Holy Ghost which is given unto him. And as long as he walketh in love, (which he may always do), he worships God in spirit and in truth. He keeps the commandments of God, and does those things that are pleasing in his sight . . . And he has power both over outward and inward sin, even from the moment he is justified.[8]

It is worth citing just one more scripture concerning how this transformation is accomplished. In his letter to the church at Ephesus, the apostle Paul wrote his strongest statement of what God had done to save sinful humanity:

> We were by nature objects of wrath. But because of his great love for us, God, who is rich in mercy, made us alive with Christ even when we were dead in transgressions—it is by grace you have been saved. And God raised us up with Christ and seated us with him in the heavenly realms in Christ Jesus, in order that in the coming ages he might show the incomparable riches of his grace, expressed in his kindness to us in Christ Jesus. For it is by grace you have been saved, through faith—and

this not from yourselves, it is the gift of God—not by works, so that no one can boast. (Ephesians 2:3*b*–9)

It is precisely because of this absolutely unwarranted, transformative gift of salvation—which makes one "alive with Christ"—that the call to Christlikeness becomes a realistic possibility.

I urge you to live a life worthy of the calling you have received. Be completely humble and gentle; be patient, bearing with one another in love. Make every effort to keep the unity of the Spirit through the bond of peace. . . . Be imitators of God, therefore, as dearly loved children and live a life of love, just as Christ loved us and gave himself up for us as a fragrant offering and sacrifice to God. (Ephesians 4:1-3; 5:1-2)

What God has done for us, and in us, makes the expectation of Christlikeness a realistic possibility. The call to holiness is not to be understood as either an oppressive legalism or dismissed as impossibility because of the transforming power of the justifying-regenerating-sanctifying grace of God.

But with all that has been written so far, the story is still incomplete. The subject of the next chapter—how God, through Christ, transforms the repentant sinner—is the most important chapter in the entire book.

8

THE GREAT PRIVILEGE OF THOSE WHO ARE BORN OF GOD

"But however it be expressed, it is certain all true faith, and the whole work
of salvation, every good thought, word, and work, is altogether by the
operation of the Spirit of God" (John Wesley).[1]

———————————◆———————————

About forty miles southeast of Dubuque, Iowa, in the hills of north-western Illinois is the small town of Stockton, which has a Nazarene church. This church was organized in 1905. It is a simple brick structure that has been remodeled throughout the years. A limestone brick set above the window facing the street has a particularly interesting engraving: "Pentecostal Church of the Nazarene." This was the name of the denomination when the church was built. However, because the denomination dropped "Pentecostal" from its name in 1919, the Stockton Church of the Nazarene hung a little cloth over that brick and, for most of the church's history, that name was hidden. In 2005, when the church celebrated its centennial, they uncovered the brick and let the name stand as it had when it had first been built. They decided they did not need to hide "Pentecostal" from the "Church of the Nazarene" any longer. If you search for the address, "178 E. Front Ave, Stockton, Illinois," you can see one of the oldest Nazarene church buildings still in use today and the only Nazarene church whose name on the building still includes the word "Pentecostal."

In its early days, the Church of the Nazarene considered "Pentecostal" an appropriate designation, since the Nazarenes emphasized the activity of the Holy Spirit in the work of salvation in general and, in particular, the "baptism of the Holy Spirit" in sanctification. But they dropped "Pentecostal" from the name in 1919 because they did not believe a baptism of the Holy Spirit was accompanied by "speaking in tongues." Thus the name was changed to avoid confusion with the growing charismatic movement. Dropping the name, however, did not lessen the recognition that the Holy Spirit is the agent of salvation. The Holy Spirit convicts of sin, enables repentance, sanctifies wholly, and provides assurance of salvation. It is the Holy Spirit who comes to live within the heart of the believer!

This explicit proclamation of the possibility of the indwelling of the Holy Spirit was one of the holiness movement's strengths and is, as might be expected, quite Wesleyan. In his essay "A Further Appeal to Men of Reason," Wesley outlined the essentials of the Christian faith to a skeptical public and of the necessity of the Holy Spirit for salvation:

> The author of faith and salvation is God alone. It is he that works in us both to will and to do. He is the sole Giver of every good gift, and the sole Author of every good work. There is no more of power than of merit in man; but as all merit is in the Son of God, in what he has done and suffered for us, so all power is in the Spirit of God. And therefore every man, in order to believe unto salvation, must receive the Holy Ghost. This is essentially necessary to every Christian, not in order to his working miracles, but in order to faith, peace, joy, and love, the ordinary fruits of the Spirit.[2]

In light of the Wesleyan-holiness emphasis on the possibility of God the Holy Spirit inhabiting his people, it is understandable that "Pentecostal" was an appropriate name for the denomination, for it was on the day of Pentecost that this historic gift of God himself was given. The Christian tradition understands that Pentecost fulfilled the Old Testament promise of God's Spirit. The prophet Isaiah, writing seven centuries before Christ, spoke of that day.

> But now listen, O Jacob, my servant, Israel, whom I have chosen.
> This is what the LORD says—
>> he who made you, who formed you in the womb,
>> and who will help you:
> Do not be afraid, O Jacob, my servant,
>> Jeshurun, whom I have chosen.

> For I will pour water on the thirsty land,
>> and streams on the dry ground;
> I will pour out my Spirit on your offspring,
>> and my blessing on your descendants.
> They will spring up like grass in a meadow,
>> like poplar trees by flowing streams. (Isaiah 44:1-4)

Isaiah was not the only prophetic voice. Ezekiel also looked forward to this gift of the indwelling of God's Spirit:

> I will take you out of the nations; I will gather you from all the countries and bring you back into your own land. I will sprinkle clean water on you, and you will be clean; I will cleanse you from all your impurities and from all your idols. I will give you a new heart and put a new spirit in you; I will remove from you your heart of stone and give you a heart of flesh. And I will put my Spirit in you and move you to follow my decrees and be careful to keep my laws. (Ezekiel 36:24-27)

On the day of Pentecost, the apostle Peter quotes the minor prophet Joel to help his hearers understand what was happening on that historic day:

> And afterward,
>> I will pour out my Spirit on all people.
> Your sons and daughters will prophesy,
>> your old men will dream dreams,
>> your young men will see visions.
> Even on my servants, both men and women,
>> I will pour out my Spirit in those days. (Joel 2:28-29)

This promise of the Holy Spirit was John the Baptist's message on the day of Jesus' baptism. John declared that the fulfillment of that prophetic promise had arrived in Jesus, who would give God's Spirit:

> I baptize you with water for repentance. But after me will come one who is more powerful than I, whose sandals I am not fit to carry. He will baptize you with the Holy Spirit and with fire. His winnowing fork is in his hand, and he will clear his threshing floor, gathering his wheat into the barn and burning up the chaff with unquenchable fire. (Matthew 3:11-12)

It is what Jesus himself promised:

> If you love me, you will obey what I command. And I will ask the Father, and he will give you another Counselor to be with you forever—the Spirit of truth. The world cannot accept him, because it neither sees him nor knows him. But you know him, for he lives with you and will be in you. I will not leave you as orphans; I will come to you. Before long, the world will not see me anymore, but you will see me. Because I live, you also will live. On that day you will realize that I am in my Father, and you are in me, and I am in you. (John 14:15-20)

Luke recorded the fulfillment of the promise in Acts:

> When the day of Pentecost came, they were all together in one place. Suddenly a sound like the blowing of a violent wind came from heaven and filled the whole house where they were sitting. They saw what seemed to be tongues of fire that separated and came to rest on each of them. All of them were filled with the Holy Spirit. (Acts 2:1-4a)

This promised fulfillment of the gift of the Holy Spirit to all those who would call on the name of the Lord was a historic event. In light of the salvation story, it should be recognized that the day of Pentecost is one of the most important days in the history of the world. Just as Christ's birth, death, resurrection, and ascension are considered historic events to the faith, so should be that fiftieth day after Christ's death. Pentecost, the descent of the Holy Spirit to those waiting and praying disciples, was understood as God fulfilling his promise through Jesus Christ. Indeed, it was Pentecost that brought to fulfillment Christ's life, death, and resurrection.

This understanding of the Holy Spirit as a gift to God's people was the clear teaching of the apostle Paul. In the letter to the church at Rome, when he wrote of the consequences of justifying faith, he mentioned through whom that grace was received:

> Therefore, since we have been justified through faith, we have peace with God through our Lord Jesus Christ, through whom we have gained access by faith into this grace in which we now stand. And we rejoice in the hope of the glory of God. Not only so, but we also rejoice in our sufferings, because we know that suffering produces perseverance;

perseverance, character; and character, hope. And hope does not disappoint us, because God has poured out his love into our hearts by the Holy Spirit, whom he has given us. (Romans 5:1-5)

In the same letter, Paul made absolutely clear the necessity of the indwelling of the Holy Spirit to followers of Jesus Christ: "And if anyone does not have the Spirit of Christ, he does not belong to Christ" (Romans 8:9*b*).

This is what Wesley taught. The Holy Spirit of God is given to every person when he or she believes, and this habitation of the Holy Spirit is what defines the believer. Christians are those who have been "baptized by the Holy Spirit." In Wesley's explanation of the Christian faith, he wrote of this promise to everyone who believes:

> "Don't you know," said St. Paul, "that you are the temple of God and that His Spirit lives in you?" "Don't you know that your bodies are the temple of the Holy Ghost, who is in you?" Again he said, "You are not controlled by the flesh but by the Spirit." Why? "The Spirit of God lives in you . . ." And St. Peter said the same: "The Spirit of glory and of God rests on you." O what comfort is this to the heart of a true Christian, to think that the Holy Ghost dwells in him! "If God be with us," as the Apostle said, "who can be against us?" He gives patience and joyfulness of heart, in temptation and affliction, and is therefore worthily called "the Comforter." (John 14:16.) He instructs the hearts of the simple in the knowledge of God and his word; therefore he is justly termed "the Spirit of truth." (John 16:13.) From this passage I learn, First, that every true Christian now "receives the Holy Ghost," as the Paraclete or Comforter promised by our Lord.[3]

While the theology of the holiness tradition identified the gift of the Holy Spirit with the moment of entire sanctification, which Wesley did not do, there was general recognition in the "Pentecostal" Church of the Nazarene of the necessary activity of the Holy Spirit for salvation from beginning to end. It was the Holy Spirit who convicted. It was the Holy Spirit who enabled a response. It was the Holy Spirit who assured of salvation. But most importantly, just as the disciples received the Holy Spirit on the day of

Pentecost, so those in the Wesleyan-holiness tradition believed that the gift of the indwelling presence of the Holy Spirit was their privilege also.

The Holy Spirit was significant for Wesley because, in addition to the biblical witness, he recognized the Holy Spirit as the source of all righteousness. To Wesley, without the presence of the Holy Spirit, even continuing in the faith would be impossible. Consequently, without the presence of the Holy Spirit, growth in grace toward Christlikeness would be impossible. Wesley wrote:

> Although no man on earth can explain the particular manner wherein the Spirit of God works on the soul, yet whosoever has these fruits, cannot but know and feel that God has wrought them in his heart.
>
> Sometimes He acts more particularly on the understanding, opening or enlightening it, (as the Scripture speaks,) and revealing, unveiling, discovering to us "the deep things of God."
>
> Sometimes He acts on the wills and affections of men; withdrawing them from evil, inclining them to good, inspiring (breathing, as it were) good thoughts into them: So it has frequently been expressed, by an easy, natural metaphor, strictly analogous to *ruach, pneuma, spiritus*, and the words used in most modern tongues also, to denote the third person in the ever-blessed Trinity. But however it be expressed, it is certain all true faith, and the whole work of salvation, every good thought, word, and work, is altogether by the operation of the Spirit of God.[4]

Without the indwelling presence of the Holy Spirit, there is no power or ability to remain, let alone, grow in faith. With the Holy Spirit, however, the believer not only remains in Christ but grows toward Christlikeness. The particular work of the Holy Spirit is nothing other than sanctification. In "A Letter to a Roman Catholic," Wesley explicitly identifies the Holy Spirit as Sanctifier:

> I believe the infinite and eternal Spirit of God, equal with the Father and Son, to be . . . the immediate cause of all holiness in us; enlightening our understandings, rectifying our wills and affections, renewing our natures, uniting our persons to Christ, assuring us of the adoption of

sons, leading us in our actions, purifying and sanctifying our souls and bodies to a full and eternal enjoyment of God.[5]

This understanding of the work of the Holy Spirit as sanctifying is not uniquely Wesleyan. The church at large has long understood the work of the Holy Spirit to be sanctification—church tradition has long accepted that God the Father is revealed as Creator, God the Son is revealed as Redeemer, and God the Holy Spirit is revealed as Sanctifier. While it is crucial to recognize that all three persons of the Trinity, by virtue of their unity, are involved in the creating, redeeming, and sanctifying process, it is not inappropriate to understand the Trinity by an appreciation of their respective "work." In his *Large Catechism,* Martin Luther identifies the Holy Spirit as the one that makes holy. Commenting on the third paragraph of the Apostles' Creed ("I believe in the Holy Ghost"), Luther writes:

> To this article, as I have said, I cannot give a better title than "Sanctification." In it is expressed and portrayed the Holy Spirit and his office, which is that he makes us holy. Therefore we must concentrate on the term "Holy Spirit," because it is so precise that we can find no substitute for it. Many other kinds of spirits are mentioned in the Scriptures, such as the spirit of man, heavenly spirits, and the evil spirit. But God's Spirit alone is called Holy Spirit, that is, he who has sanctified and still sanctifies us. For as the Father is called Creator and the Son is called Redeemer, so on account of his work the Holy Spirit must be called Sanctifier, the one who makes holy.[6]

The Reformed Westminster Confession of Faith recognizes the work of the Holy Spirit to be sanctifying. Under the Article of Faith titled "Sanctification," these Presbyterian clergymen wrote:

> Although the remaining corruption [of sin], for a time may much prevail, yet, through the continual supply of strength from the sanctifying Spirit of Christ, the regenerate part doth overcome; and so the saints grow in grace, perfecting holiness in the fear of God.[7]

The Church of the Nazarene's third article of faith—"The Holy Spirit" —describes this particular work.

3. We believe in the Holy Spirit, the Third Person of the Triune God-head, that He is ever present and efficiently active in and with the Church of Christ, convincing the world of sin, regenerating those who repent and believe, sanctifying believers, and guiding into all truth as it is in Jesus.[8]

As a matter of fact, some contemporary baptismal rituals, in an effort to move away from gender-specific language, are even substituting the traditional Trinitarian formula, "In the Name of the Father, Son, and Spirit," with "In the Name of the Creator, Redeemer, and Sanctifier," acknowledging their distinctive roles. Regardless, understanding the Holy Spirit as the one who sanctifies is universal among all theological traditions.

The presence of the Holy Spirit in the life of the believer makes justification transformative and holiness possible. The justification of the sinner, which Christ provided for through his shed blood, has resulted in the gift of the Holy Spirit, who continues the redemptive work of God in the present age by sanctifying the justified!

The title of this chapter is the title of Wesley's sermon "The Great Privilege of Those Who Are Born of God." The reasons for the selection of this particular sermon as the title for a chapter on the gift of the Holy Spirit are two. The first is what Wesley considered the privilege of those born of God: God's justifying grace is so transformative, due to the Holy Spirit, that it enables the justified to "not commit sin." This harmonizes with the apostle Paul's letter to the church at Rome:

Therefore, there is now no condemnation for those who are in Christ Jesus, because through Christ Jesus the law of the Spirit of life set me free from the law of sin and death. For what the law was powerless to do in that it was weakened by the sinful nature, God did by sending his own Son in the likeness of sinful man to be a sin offering. And so he condemned sin in sinful man, in order that the righteous requirements of the law might be fully met in us, who do not live according to the sinful nature but according to the Spirit. (Romans 8:1-4)

This indicates that the righteous requirements of the law can be fully met precisely because of Christ's atonement and the subsequent gift of the

Holy Spirit. Greathouse and Lyons agree with this in their commentary on this passage:

> Christ fulfilled the law for us that it might be fulfilled in us. The love that moved him to obey the Father and give himself for others now empowers . . . What makes all the difference in the new situation is that the indwelling Spirit now displaces indwelling Sin. The indwelling Spirit is the power of new life in Christ. God has made good his promise to write the Law upon the hearts of his people and through the Spirit to grant the capacity to obey his law.[9]

So the righteous requirements of the law can be fully met precisely because of Christ's atonement and the subsequent gift of the Holy Spirit. Justification provides freedom from the power of sin, and this leads to holiness. Thus, holiness is possible because of what God the Holy Spirit accomplishes in the life of the believer, and not because of anything the believer accomplishes alone.

The second reason for selecting this particular sermon for a chapter title is Wesley's careful recognition of the dynamic nature of the work of the Holy Spirit. Wesley did not take this promise of the Holy Spirit's presence as some sort of static possession, but understood it as the dynamic, overwhelming life of God with—and within—the believer. It is probably just as accurate to say that the Holy Spirit possesses the believer as it is to say the believer possesses the Holy Spirit! This "baptism of the Holy Spirit" is not simply a one-time event, but the continuous pouring out of the life of God. Wesley, borrowing the New Testament metaphor, likened the Holy Spirit in the believer to breath. The Holy Spirit is breathed into the justified and sanctified believer and the fruit of that Spirit's life is breathed back to God in holiness. From the sermon that is the title of this chapter, Wesley wrote:

> From what has been said, we may learn, secondly, what the life of God in the soul of a believer is; wherein it properly consists; and what is immediately and necessarily implied therein. It immediately and necessarily implies the continual inspiration of God's Holy Spirit; God's breathing into the soul, and the soul's breathing back what it first receives from God; a continual action of God upon the soul, and a re-

action of the soul upon God; an unceasing presence of God, the loving, pardoning God, manifested to the heart, and perceived by faith; and an unceasing return of love, praise, and prayer, offering up all the thoughts of our hearts, all the words of our tongues, all the works of our hands, all our body, soul, and spirit, to be a holy sacrifice, acceptable unto God in Christ Jesus.[10]

The possibility of living without sin is due to the presence of the Holy Spirit, who is always being poured out into the lives of believers. This gift of the Holy Spirit is not a magical power somehow infused into the believer but is rather the vibrant life of the personal God who gives himself to the justified believer and on whom the believer depends. In other words, the gift of the personal presence of the Holy Spirit ought to be considered not only as a past event received at justification but also as a continuous and contemporary gift. This continuous gift of God's Spirit enables the life of holiness. Love, joy, peace, patience, kindness, goodness, faithfulness, gentleness, and self-control are all the result of the life of the Holy Spirit of God within and among God's people. (See Galatians 5:22-25.)

In an effort to remind people of this incredible promise of the gift of God himself, I have asked them this simple question: *When did you receive the Holy Spirit?* It is a variation of Paul's question to the believers in Ephesus (Acts 19:2): "Did you receive the Holy Spirit when you believed?" If anyone had asked that of the apostles, they would have been able to answer definitively (2:14-18). If those converted by Peter's preaching on the day of Pentecost had been asked, they would have been able to answer definitively (v. 38). If the Samaritans converted by Philip had been asked, they would have been able to answer definitively (8:17). If the apostle Paul had been asked, he would have been able to answer definitively (9:17). Indeed, if any of the believers in the book of Acts had been asked, they would have known the answer. Granting that the book of Acts is a record of historical events and therefore not to be interpreted as everyone's experience with the Holy Spirit, most Christians should be able to answer the question concerning the indwelling of the Spirit.

But my experience suggests otherwise. I asked that question to board members in a small Nazarene church several years ago, and they didn't know how to answer. I have asked that question of students in my Doctrine of Holiness class. Granted, some of them are afraid to answer because they think it is some sort of a trick question, and some don't want to give a wrong answer; but in truth, by the looks on some of their faces, some of them could say what the church at Ephesus said to the apostle Paul: "No, we have not even heard that there is a Holy Spirit." I asked that question when I preached at Olivet's College Church of the Nazarene in Bourbonnais. Following the sermon, a person who had been a Nazarene a long time came up to me with tears in his eyes, thanking me for letting him know that God the Holy Spirit was dwelling within him. He evidently had forgotten or had never known the promise of Christ to his people.

Now, there are many reasons why some are not able to answer definitively that they were gifted with the Holy Spirit at justification, and one shouldn't draw too strong a conclusion from anecdotal evidence. With that said, there seems to be a poverty of preaching and teaching and most importantly a poverty of experiential knowledge of the incredible gift of the Holy Spirit, the reason for Christ's life, death, and resurrection. As a consequence, we risk attributing salvation to ourselves and we risk disbelieving that holiness is possible.

The Church of the Nazarene in Stockton, Illinois, has carved in stone on their building the name "The Pentecostal Church of the Nazarene," today visible for all to see. The name of the church, at least for a short time, reflected the priority the denomination gave to the Holy Spirit's sanctifying power. However, for much of the Stockton church's history, a cloth hid that "Pentecostal" name from sight. It has been only in the last several years that they uncovered the name to the community. In light of the incredible gift of the Holy Spirit to everyone who believes, and in light of the work of the Holy Spirit making God's people Christlike, it would be helpful for the holiness tradition at large and the Church of the Nazarene in particular to do as that Stockton church has done. Uncovering the "Pentecostal" heritage of the holiness movement would make it crystal clear that holiness is not something achieved but rather Someone received.

LOVE

9

THE REPENTANCE OF BELIEVERS

"When our Lord and Master, Jesus Christ, said 'Repent,' He called for the entire life of believers to be one of repentance" (Martin Luther).[1]

In Wesleyan-holiness churches in the twentieth century, one of the most important pieces of liturgical furniture was the altar. Placed in front of the sanctuary between the congregation and raised platform, the altar was a simple bench or rail, a place to kneel and pray for salvation or consecration. The opportunity to do this usually occurred at the end of the sermon, when the pastor or evangelist would encourage people to come forward to confess and commit. The altar call was so integral to the identity of the holiness movement that it was common for mid-twentieth-century holiness churches to hold altar calls at the conclusion of almost every service. In addition, pastors faithfully scheduled revival services twice a year, whose sole purpose was to provide opportunities for people to repent and consecrate themselves at the altar. The altar call was so central to the service that the effectiveness of preaching was often measured by how many responded to the invitation. For many in the holiness tradition, the invitation to the altar was the primary sacrament.

This liturgical practice was particularly appropriate to the holiness movement due to the emphasis on consecration—the grace of entire sanctification was only possible through this. The Article of Faith in the Church of the Nazarene that explains entire sanctification indicates this dependence. In words that have remained substantially unchanged from the very beginning of the denomination's history, it states: "Entire sanctification is provided by the blood of Jesus, is wrought instantaneously by faith, [and] preceded by entire consecration."[2] In the holiness movement, when someone commits entirely to the discerned will of God, desires nothing other than what God desires, relinquishes every trace of self-sovereignty, then he or she is entirely sanctified. The hymns that were used as invitations to the altar reinforced this requirement of consecration for this second work of grace. One such hymn was written by Judson Wheeler Van DeVenter, a Methodist evangelist, whose affection for the song was so strong that he requested its title carved on his tombstone. He wrote and holiness people sang:

> All to Jesus, I surrender;
>> All to Him I freely give;
> I will ever love and trust Him,
>> In His presence daily live.
>
> All to Jesus I surrender;
>> Humbly at His feet I bow,
> Worldly pleasures all forsaken;
>> Take me, Jesus, take me now.
>
> All to Jesus, I surrender;
>> Lord, I give myself to Thee;
> Fill me with Thy love and power;
>> Let Thy blessing fall on me.
>
> I surrender all,
> I surrender all,
> All to Thee, my blessed Savior,
> I surrender all.[3]

Elisha Hoffman, a Presbyterian pastor and prolific songwriter, wrote another popular holiness hymn that refers to the altar as the place of consecration. "Is Your All on the Altar?" was written in 1905 and made familiar again by the gospel artist Yolanda Adams. The message of this song denotes the relationship between consecration at an altar of prayer and a life of full salvation:

> You have longed for sweet peace,
> And for faith to increase,
>> And have earnestly, fervently prayed;

But you cannot have rest,
Or be perfectly blest,
    Until all on the altar is laid.

Would you walk with the Lord,
In the light of His Word,
    And have peace and contentment alway?
You must do His sweet will,
To be free from all ill,
    On the altar your all you must lay.

O we never can know
What the Lord will bestow
    Of the blessings for which we have prayed,
Till our body and soul
He doth fully control,
    And our all on the altar is laid.

Refrain:
Is your all on the altar of sacrifice laid?
    Your heart does the Spirit control?
You can only be blest,
And have peace and sweet rest,
    As you yield Him your body and soul.[4]

It is the experience of those in the holiness tradition that a critical change occurs in the life of the believer when he or she makes a conscious decision to surrender completely and consecrate his or her life entirely to the acknowledged will of God. This change is so significant that it is difficult to interpret it in any other way than entirely sanctifying. As a matter of fact, it was so decisive for so many that it was common to hear testimonies of the exact time and place such consecrations for entire sanctification were made.

The justification for calling Christians to a complete consecration after committing to Christ is found in the repeated calls in the New Testament for those of faith to commit themselves again and anew. Chapter 6 already referenced scriptures that repeat the call for the believer to participate in

God's sanctifying grace through obedience and consecration. For example, the apostle Paul wrote to the church at Corinth:

> Since we have these promises, dear friends, let us purify ourselves from everything that contaminates body and spirit, perfecting holiness out of reverence for God. (2 Corinthians 7:1)

Again to the church at Ephesus:

> You were taught, with regard to your former way of life, to put off your old self, which is being corrupted by its deceitful desires; to be made new in the attitude of your minds; and to put on the new self, created to be like God in true righteousness and holiness. (Ephesians 4:22-24)

However, the scripture that provides the clearest justification for a call to consecration after justification is found in Romans. After writing to believers of all that God had done for them, Paul wrote:

> Therefore, I urge you, brothers, in view of God's mercy, to offer your bodies as living sacrifices, holy and pleasing to God—this is your spiritual act of worship. Do not conform any longer to the pattern of this world, but be transformed by the renewing of your mind. Then you will be able to test and approve what God's will is—his good, pleasing and perfect will. (Romans 12:1-2)

Holiness theologians understand this passage as a call for complete consecration. While it certainly includes the idea of maintaining an attitude of sacrificial service in response to God's grace, it also indicates the need for a conscious decision to submit to God's will. In their commentary on the book of Romans, William Greathouse and George Lyons interpret this passage as a call to a specific, entirely sanctifying consecration:

> The tense of the infinitive "to offer" and the logic of sacrificial imagery . . . call for a decisive, once-for-all consecration that is to be perpetually sustained, not repeatedly retracted and returned.[5]

A few pages later, commenting on that same verse, they write: "Justified persons are called to consecrate themselves unreservedly to God. This total surrender to God is the necessary human condition for entire sanctification."[6]

In addition to the calls to consecration illustrated by Paul's letters, there are biblical examples of those who intentionally and specifically submitted themselves to the will of God. Mary, the mother of Jesus, serves as an example. When told she was going to be the mother of the Savior of the world, she responded with this powerful prayer of submission: "I am the Lord's servant . . . May it be to me as you have said" (Luke 1:38). Jesus himself, in the garden of Gethsemane on the eve of his crucifixion, prayed the difficult prayer of resignation: "Yet not my will, but yours be done" (Luke 22:42). Indeed, Jesus indicated that submission to, and participation in, the will of God was expected of all his followers, for he instructed them to pray this comprehensive third petition of the Lord's Prayer: "Your will be done on earth as it is in heaven" (Matthew 6:10). Evidently, there is biblical precedent for making a decisive and complete consecration to the revealed will of God.

However, this kind of consecration is not an easy decision and therefore should not be made without much consideration and forethought. Indeed, one of the reasons it is so decisive is precisely because it is so encompassing. The believer is doing nothing less than offering himself or herself sacrificially and without reservation to the good, pleasing, and perfect will of God.

John Wesley recognized the need for the will to be in full harmony with, and submissive to, the will of God for the sake of holiness, and it became a major theme in his writings. In the sermon that is the title of this chapter, in which he illustrated the need for the continuing and decisive work of sanctification, Wesley wrote of the sin that still needed cleansing from the hearts of believers. He specifically identified as needing sanctifying the will that was contrary to God's will:

> Nor is it long before [the believer] feels *self-will in his heart,* even a will contrary to the will of God. A will every man must inevitably have, as long as he has an understanding. This is an essential part of human nature, indeed of the nature of every intelligent being. Our blessed Lord himself had a will as a man; otherwise he had not been a man. But his human will was invariably subject to the will of his Father. At all times, and on all occasions, even in the deepest affliction, he could say, *"Not as I will, but as thou wilt."* But this is not the case at all times, even with a true believer in Christ. He frequently finds his will more or less exalting itself against the will of God. He wills something, because

it is pleasing to nature, which is not pleasing to God. And he [doesn't will] something because it is painful to nature, which is the will of God concerning him. Indeed (suppose he continues in the faith) he fights against it with all his might. But this very thing implies that it really exists, and that he is conscious of it.[7]

The significance of a submissive will for the sake of holiness can be easily seen in Wesley's sermon titled "On Obedience to Parents," written when he was eighty-one years old. Using the scripture from Colossians 3:20, where Paul gives concise instruction for children to obey their parents, Wesley explains the necessity for parents to enforce obedience precisely because submission was so crucial for holiness. In rather unequivocal language, he wrote:

I cannot yet dismiss this subject. *As self-will is the root of all sin and misery,* so whatever cherishes this in children ensures their after-wretchedness and irreligion; and whatever checks and mortifies it promotes their future happiness and piety. This is still more evident if we consider that religion is nothing else but the doing the will of God, and not our own; and that *self-will being the grand impediment to our temporal and eternal happiness,* no indulgence of it can be trivial; no denial of it unprofitable. Heaven or hell depends on this alone. So that the parent who studies to subdue it in his children works together with God in the saving of a soul. The parent who indulges it does the devil's work, makes religion impracticable, salvation unattainable, and does all that in him lies to damn his child, soul and body, forever![8]

In his sermon "Circumcision of the Heart" Wesley describes holiness as humility, faith, hope, and love; he concludes with a paragraph alluding both to Romans 12 and Jesus' prayer of consecration to the will of God:

Here, then, is the sum of the perfect law; this is the true circumcision of the heart . . . Other sacrifices from us he would not [have]; but the living sacrifice of the heart he has chosen. Let it be continually offered up to God through Christ, in flames of holy love. And let no creature be suffered to share with him: For He is a jealous God. His throne He will not divide with another: He will reign without a rival . . . "Have a pure intention of heart, a steadfast regard to his glory in all your actions." "Fix your eye upon the blessed hope of your calling, and make all the things of the world minister unto it." *For then, and not till then* is that "mind in us which was also in Christ Jesus;" when, in every motion of our heart, in every word of our tongue, in every work of our hands, we "pursue nothing but in relation to him, and in subordination to his pleasure;" when we, too, neither think, nor speak, nor act, *to fulfill our* "own will, but the will of him that sent us;" when, whether we eat, or drink, or whatever we do, we do all to the glory of God.[9]

In light of the consistent call in the Bible for believers to "offer themselves as living sacrifices" subsequent to justification; in light of the Wesleyan-holiness emphasis on the need for the human will to be in full conformity to the will of God for salvation to be completed; and in light of the examples of those who have done so, it is easy to see how the revivalistic practice of "going to the altar" to make a complete consecration took priority in the process of salvation. Most Christians, regardless of theological tradition, recognize what Wesley pointed out in his sermon "The Repentance of Believers"—having a will in perfect submission to the will of God is not always the case for even the most earnest Christians, and coming to complete consecration is an important milestone in the spiritual pilgrimage.

The understandable and appropriate call to consecration for sanctification lent itself to a rather static interpretation of salvation. When one made a complete consecration, one was entirely sanctified; this seemed to be popularly understood as meaning that the sanctifying work of God was mostly done! With such emphasis placed on consecration, the inadvertent message was that believers need only "get entirely sanctified" to become holy and thus arrive at that relatively finished state. The experience of consecration, which is decisive and transformative, became for many the primary assurance that one had met the demands of holiness. In other words, the "experience" of consecration became the proof of holiness. When one entirely consecrated, one had arrived.

The danger with this understanding of entire sanctification is obvious. If one believes the sanctifying work of God is completed in a second work of grace—contingent upon consecration—one can be deluded into thinking further repentance or consecration is unnecessary.

Understanding entire sanctification as the completion of God's work in the life of the believer could, in fact, lead to the abortion of God's continued sanctifying work; by this definition, any further sanctifying work by the Holy Spirit would be unnecessary. I will never forget the response of a young man whose mother testified to entire sanctification as a teenager and who, in her words, had not sinned since. He replied, "But I lived with her." As far as he was concerned, the experience of entire sanctification was discredited.

The misunderstanding that entire sanctification means that God's sanctifying work is completed and that no further growth or maturation is possible is illustrated by my repeated experiences with students in my Doctrine of Holiness classes. The majority of these young people are ministerial students working toward licensure and ordination in the Church of the Nazarene. On the ministerial license application form for the Church of the Nazarene is this question: "Are you entirely sanctified?" On that same form, the applicant is asked to provide a description of the occasion of his or her entire sanctification. Some students are reluctant to answer "yes" because they interpret that question to mean something like, "Has God finished his work in you?" or "Are you perfectly holy?" or "Are you spiritually mature?" Interpreting the question like that obviously inclines the students to answer "no" to the question, even though he or she is afraid such an answer will put the licensing in jeopardy.

The holiness tradition has a long history of clarifying this question and a long history of distinguishing between "purity of intention" and "maturity of character." The question, "Are you entirely sanctified?" was not, and is not, intended to ask if God's sanctifying work has been completed, nor is it intended to ask about complete maturity in the faith. Entire sanctification, as understood in the Church of the Nazarene today, refers, not to having been made perfect in love, as Wesley understood it, but to singleness of intention. The question, "Are you entirely sanctified?" is asking whether or not someone has completely consecrated his or her life to the understood will of God. The question, "Are you entirely sanctified?" is asking whether or not one has prayed as authentically as what Jesus prayed in the garden: "Yet not my will, but yours be done" (Luke 22:42). When I explain to my ministerial students that the question on the ministerial application is not asking if God's work is completed in their life but is rather asking if they have committed themselves entirely to Christ and his sanctifying work, those who have made such a commitment are more than willing to answer "yes." Indeed, they find it easy to testify to God's continuously (entirely) sanctifying work and many can point to the occasion when they made a complete consecration.

There are some in the holiness tradition who think we ought to drop that question in the application precisely because it leads to a too-static interpretation of God's sanctifying work, and because the church is not asking about having been perfected in love, but about consecration. Questions more dynamic in nature are suggested. I have heard the recommendation to use the questions that the United Methodist church asks in their ministerial application: "Are you going on to perfection?" and "Do you expect to be made perfect in love in this life?"[10] Another recommendation allows for a more dynamic understanding of sanctification: "Are you being entirely sanctified?"

At this point, it is important to note that the phrase "entire sanctification" was not created by those in the holiness tradition but was originally derived from the apostle Paul's prayer at the end of his first letter to the church at Thessalonica:

> Now may the God of peace Himself sanctify you entirely; and may your spirit and soul and body be preserved complete, without blame at the coming of our Lord Jesus Christ. Faithful is He who calls you, and He also will bring it to pass. (1 Thessalonians 5:23-24, NASB)

John Wesley used the particular term on significant occasions. In the sermon that is the title of this chapter, he lamented the general lack of interest in entire sanctification due to the unawareness of the sin that still corrupted believers, and the general disbelief in the possibility of holiness. He wrote:

> Hence it is that those believers who are not convinced of the deep corruption of their hearts, or but slightly and as it were nominally convinced, have little concern about *entire sanctification*. They may possibly hold the opinion that such a thing is to be, either at death, or some

time (they know not when) before it. But they have no great uneasiness for the want of it, and no great hunger or thirst after it. They cannot, until they know themselves better, until they repent.[11]

The question concerning whether or not one has been "entirely sanctified" is thus derived from the apostle Paul's particular prayer in 1 Thessalonians 5 and from John Wesley's unapologetic use of the term. However, the Thessalonians prayer and Wesley's reference do not refer primarily to consecration, but to the sanctifying work of the Holy Spirit, which culminates in Christlikeness. When Wesley asked the question, he was not referring to consecration; he was referring to having been perfected in love!

Regardless of its merit on the ministerial application, the question as Paul prayed it, and as John Wesley understood it, is an important one for all Christians to consider. As Wesley wrote, it compels people to take seriously the expectation of holiness and the possibility of its realization, through the grace of God, in this world. In light of the general indifference, and even rejection, of the possibility among contemporary Christians, John Wesley's plea for full salvation in that same sermon is as relevant today as it was in 1767:

> Believe the glad tidings of great salvation, which God hath prepared for all people. Believe that He who is "the brightness of his Father's glory, the express image of his person," is "able to save unto the uttermost all that come unto God through him." He is able to save you from all the sin that still remains in your heart. He is able to save you from all the sin that cleaves to all your words and actions. He is able to save you from sins of omission, and to supply whatever is wanting in you. It is true, this is impossible with man; but with God-Man all things are possible. For what can be too hard for him who hath "all power in heaven and in earth"?[12]

The question whether or not one has been entirely sanctified is important for another reason. In addition to pointing out the possibility of holiness, the question calls for a commitment to pursuing holiness, or Christlikeness, in a way that other variations of the question do not. The question, "Are you entirely sanctified?" understood as a call for consecration, is helpful because it recognizes that consecration to Christ for sanctification subsequent to justification is, after all, sanctifying in a profoundly significant way. This is why the holiness movement placed sacramental significance on the altar call and did not apologize for calling people to make the difficult decision to give themselves entirely over to the will of God, even as fully as Christ had done.

There are numerous examples of believers who can testify to the decisively sanctifying nature of entire consecration. I have already spoken of my repeated consecrations in chapter 5. As a pastor and professor, I have been, and am witness to, many who, often at an altar of prayer, surrender their lives to the will of God and whose Christian lives are qualitatively different as a consequence. But one of the most intriguing times that I have witnessed occurred in Kansas City several years ago. I was privileged to be a part of a theological dialogue group that included a general leader in the Church of the Nazarene, a president of one of the denomination's academic institutions, several professors of different denominational universities, pastors of various Nazarene churches, and a few people who worked at the denominational headquarters. We had spent the morning and early afternoon in guided conversation about the theological issues facing the North American-holiness tradition. Among other things, we had talked about the Wesleyan and American-holiness distinctives and the relative strengths and weaknesses of each of them. We talked about the history and the present state of the holiness movement. It was all very academic and theoretical and, to theologians, rather compelling. I am not sure what prompted what happened next, but one of the individuals said that they would like to share their "entire sanctification" experience. While we had been talking about holiness in general, we hadn't been talking about the "experience" of entire sanctification in particular, so it was a rather abrupt transition. We were anxious to hear what he had to say, and he talked about a moment of consecration that was decisive and transformative. Immediately after he told his story, another person said, "I'd like to share my entire sanctification story too." Following that person, another shared a story, and then another, and then another. For the next hour or so, I was privileged to hear wonderful experiences of God's sanctifying grace at a moment of consecration from theologians who were all acutely aware of the theological deficiencies and common misunderstandings of holiness theology. But with one request to share a personal testimony, we went from an academic classroom to a cottage prayer meeting. While none of them claimed to having been completely perfected at that moment, according to the testimonies of those people around the table that afternoon, consecrating their lives to the revealed will of God was sanctifying.

As mentioned before, this emphasis on consecration lent a too-static interpretation of the process of salvation and to a general neglect of the several means of grace to sustain the life of holiness, which will be the subject of the next chapter. Because of this, there has been a general depreciation in recent days of the need for consecration for the sake of God's sanctifying work. This has not been helpful. Obviously, this intentional decisive surrender to the revealed will of God need not take place on an altar at the end of a church service, but the testimony of the Scriptures, tradition, and experience indicate its necessity at some place, at some time in the life of the believer, and it is certainly not the end of God's continuing sanctifying work. Those altar calls provided opportunities for serious reflection, significant repentance, and subsequent consecrations. There have been people who testified to having made a complete consecration, repented, and reconsecrated; however, this was one of the strengths of the holiness movement, because a consecration to the revealed will of God is sanctifying, no matter how many times it is done! In practice, those repeated calls to surrender encouraged and provided occasions for the continuing repentance of sincere believers, both of which are crucial to the life of holiness.

In light of the extravagance of God's merciful gift of full salvation, offering ourselves as living sacrifices in response to his grace is our only reasonable response.

10

THE MEANS OF GRACE

Extra ecclesiam nulla salvator
"Outside the Church there is no salvation."

---◆---

In the *Manual of the Church of the Nazarene,* the ritual for receiving members into the church has remained essentially unchanged since the denomination's beginning. The membership ritual begins with a paragraph that speaks of the benefit of, and need for participation in, the life of the church. It reads:

> DEARLY BELOVED: The privileges and blessings that we have in association together in the Church of Jesus Christ are very sacred and precious. There is in it such hallowed fellowship as cannot otherwise be known. There is such helpfulness with brotherly watch care and counsel as can be found only in the Church. There is the godly care of pastors, with the teachings of the Word; and the helpful inspiration of social worship. And there is cooperation in service, accomplishing that which cannot otherwise be done.[1]

This short paragraph explicitly acknowledges in three separate places the uniqueness of the church for spiritual growth and accomplishment of the mission of God. The fellowship necessary for the Christian life, according to this paragraph, "cannot otherwise be known" apart from the church. The discipline and encouragement necessary for continued growth can "only be found in the Church." The fulfillment of the mission of God "cannot . . . be done" through any other institution than the church. It is an interestingly strong statement that more than implies the necessity of the church for salvation.

Those desiring to join the Church of the Nazarene are then asked three questions. The first asks for agreement with the doctrines of the Church of the Nazarene, including acknowledging the possibility of entire sanctification. The second asks for testimony to an experiential knowledge of Jesus Christ as present Savior. The third is a series of related questions in which the person is asked to commit himself or herself to the local body of believers in very particular ways:

> Desiring to unite with the Church of the Nazarene, do you covenant to give yourself to the fellowship and work of God in connection with it? Will you endeavor in every way to glorify God, by a humble walk, godly conversation, and holy service; by devotedly giving of your means; by faithful attendance upon the means of grace; and, abstaining from all evil, will you seek earnestly to perfect holiness of heart and life in the fear of the Lord?[2]

According to the membership ritual of the Church of the Nazarene, perfecting the holiness of heart and life is contingent on participation in the life of the general church—and then as a part of that community—on humility, godly conversation, participation in ministry, stewardship, and, in particular, faithfulness to the means of grace. Growing in Christlikeness is not an individual endeavor but is rather recognized as a communal responsibility. Participation in the life of the church is absolutely essential for perfecting holiness, and the clear implication of this covenantal agreement is that without this kind of faithfulness to the church, Christlikeness is impossible.

The expectations of the early Nazarenes to the church illustrate that this was more than mere formality. For most of the twentieth century, the typical Nazarene church provided a Sunday school for all ages on the first day of the week, followed by a morning worship service. The significance of these small discipleship groups to the life of the church is evidenced by the fact that more people usually attended Sunday school than the morning worship service. Sunday night was an evangelistic service that often included public testimonies of the work of God in people's lives, and which usually ended with an altar call to receive salvation or to be entirely sanctified. The midweek Wednesday evening service was a "prayer meeting," with testimonies, gospel hymns or choruses, a short Bible study, and a lengthy time of prayer. Sometimes people would pray out loud all at the same time. Sometimes they would gather at the altar and take turns praying publicly. Sometimes they would kneel at their pews. Whatever the method, Wednesday night meetings were devoted primarily to prayer. Granted, not everyone who came on Sunday morning came Sunday night, and not everyone who came Sunday night would come on Wednesday night, but the expectation—explicitly or implicitly expressed—was that if a Christian really loved the Lord, he or she was there "every time the church doors were open." In addition to these corporate gatherings, weekly "prayer and fasting" in private was encouraged for the sake of the mission. Commitment cards for prayer and fasting were distributed and collected regularly. Weekday evenings were given to visiting the sick, including the unconverted, in addition to Saturday morning prayer breakfasts and Bible study. Financial support of the church and her mission was expected from all members, and giving 10 percent of personal income to the church was considered the bare minimum. In addition to the weekly services and commitments, special services were conducted throughout the year. In the spring and fall, itinerant evangelists would speak in weeklong (or two, or three!) revivals with special emphasis given to calling people to holiness.

For Nazarenes, believers were expected to orient their lives around the church in ways the membership ritual made clear. Perfecting "holiness of heart and life in the fear of the Lord" was understood as impossible apart from the covenantal life of the church.

The necessity of the church for salvation has been understood across all theological traditions from the beginnings of Christianity. After all, it was Jesus himself who established the church. According to the gospel of Matthew, Jesus replied to Peter confessing him as the Christ by saying:

> Blessed are you, Simon son of Jonah, for this was not revealed to you by man, but by my Father in heaven. And I tell you that you are Peter, and on this rock I will build my church, and the gates of Hades will not overcome it. I will give you the keys of the kingdom of heaven; what-

ever you bind on earth will be bound in heaven, and whatever you loose on earth will be loosed in heaven. (Matthew 16:17-19)

The apostle Luke reported on the sacrificially communal nature of the Christian life throughout the book of Acts. The very first description of the church is found at the end of the second chapter:

They devoted themselves to the apostles' teaching and to the fellowship, to the breaking of bread and to prayer. Everyone was filled with awe, and many wonders and miraculous signs were done by the apostles. All the believers were together and had everything in common. Selling their possessions and goods, they gave to anyone as he had need. Every day they continued to meet together in the temple courts. They broke bread in their homes and ate together with glad and sincere hearts, praising God and enjoying the favor of all the people. And the Lord added to their number daily those who were being saved. (Acts 2:42-47)

The apostle Paul used several metaphors for the church, all indicating its necessity for the Christian life. The most familiar is the church as the body of Christ. In 1 Corinthians 12, he indicated that every person who confessed Christ as Lord and who had received the gift of the Holy Spirit was necessarily a part of the church, which is Christ's "body":

The body is a unit, though it is made up of many parts; and though all its parts are many, they form one body. So it is with Christ. For we were all baptized by one Spirit into one body—whether Jews or Greeks, slave or free—and we were all given the one Spirit to drink. . . . Now you are the body of Christ, and each one of you is a part of it. (Vv. 12-13, 27)

In 1 Corinthians 5, the apostle Paul recommended that the church at Corinth excommunicate a sexually immoral man. This was for the redemptive purpose of revealing to that man the nature of his sin and sin's inevitable consequences, all in the hopes that he might return to the church chastened and chaste. The clear implication of this passage was that incorporation into the life of the church was absolutely essential for that man's salvation. In other words, his salvation was contingent on returning to the church!

In another powerful metaphor, the apostle Paul likened the relationship between Christ and the church to that between a wife and the husband who gives his life for her. In a passage that has more to say about Christ's essential union with the church than about a marriage relationship, Paul writes:

Husbands, love your wives, just as Christ loved the church and gave himself up for her to make her holy, cleansing her by the washing with water through the word, and to present her to himself as a radiant church, without stain or wrinkle or any other blemish, but holy and blameless. In this same way, husbands ought to love their wives as their own bodies. He who loves his wife loves himself. After all, no one ever hated his own body, but he feeds and cares for it, just as Christ does the church—for we are members of his body. "For this reason a man will leave his father and mother and be united to his wife, and the two will become one flesh." This is a profound mystery—but I am talking about Christ and the church. (Ephesians 5:25-32)

The apostle Paul was evidently asserting that Christ and the church, in some inexplicable way, have become one flesh! However we understand this passage, the intimate union between Christ and his church is clear.

In that same letter, the apostle Paul made very clear the relationship between participation in the life of the church and growth in grace. Again, he identified the church as the body of Christ:

It was he who gave some to be apostles, some to be prophets, some to be evangelists, and some to be pastors and teachers, to prepare God's people for works of service, so that the body of Christ may be built up until we all reach unity in the faith and in the knowledge of the Son of God and become mature, attaining to the whole measure of the fullness of Christ. (Ephesians 4:11-13)

It was not a leap, therefore, for the early church fathers to declare that salvation was not possible outside the church. Granting the exceptional case, they made it clear that unity with, and participation in the life of the church, was expected. Irenaeus, an early church father in the second century, wrote about this issue in *Against Heresies*:

"For in the Church," it is said, "God has placed apostles, prophets, teachers," and all the other means through which the Spirit works; of whom all are not partakers who do not join themselves to the Church, but defraud themselves of life through their perverse opinions and infamous behavior. For where the Church is, there is the Spirit of God; and where the Spirit of God is, there is the Church and every kind of grace.[3]

Origen, another early church father, wrote: "Let no man deceive himself. Outside this house, that is, outside the Church no one is saved."[4] St. Cyprian, a third-century bishop and writer, reiterated these convictions: "No one can have God as Father who does not have the Church as Mother."[5]

It might be surprising that Protestant reformers also insisted on this idea. Obviously, they rejected that the Roman Catholic Church was necessary for salvation. With their minimalist definition of the church—the congregation where the Word was rightly preached and the sacraments rightly administered—they still held to the essential necessity of the church for salvation. Luther, in his *Personal Prayer Book* of 1522, wrote:

> I believe that throughout the whole wide world there is only one holy, universal, Christian church, which is nothing other than the gathering or congregation of saints—pious believers on earth. This church is gathered, preserved, and governed by the same Holy Spirit and is given daily increase by means of the sacraments and the word of God. I believe that no one can be saved who is not in this gathering or community harmoniously sharing the same faith with it, the same word, sacraments, hope, and love . . . I believe that there is forgiveness of sin nowhere else than in this community and that beyond it nothing can help to gain it—no good deeds no matter how many or how great they might be: and that within this community nothing can invalidate this forgiveness.[6]

John Calvin echoed this in his magisterial *Institutes of the Christian Religion*, published in 1599:

> As it is now our purpose to discourse of the visible Church, let us learn, from her single title of Mother, how useful, nay, how necessary the knowledge of her is, since there is no other means of entering into

life unless she conceive us in the womb and give us birth, unless she nourish us at her breasts, and, in short, keep us under her charge and government, until, divested of mortal flesh, we become like the angels . . . Beyond the pale of the Church no forgiveness of sins, no salvation can be hoped for . . . The paternal favor of God and the special evidence of spiritual life are confined to his peculiar people, and hence the abandonment of the Church is always fatal.[7]

The Seventeenth Westminster Confession of Faith, an explication of Reformed doctrines, contains this article titled "Of the Church":

The visible Church, which is also catholic or universal under the Gospel . . . consists of all those throughout the world that profess the true religion; and of their children: and is the kingdom of the Lord Jesus Christ, the house and family of God, out of which there is no ordinary possibility of salvation. (Chapter XXV, Article II)[8]

While John Wesley held to a more elastic understanding of the nature of the church,[9] he too believed that participation in the life of a community of faith was absolutely essential for the Christian. He wrote that God's people should love the church with ardent devotion:

Every Christian ought undoubtedly to be zealous for the church, bearing a strong affection to it, and earnestly desiring its prosperity and increase. He ought to be thus zealous, as for the church universal, praying for it continually, so especially for that particular church or Christian society whereof he himself is a member. For this he ought to wrestle with God in prayer; meantime using every means in his power to enlarge its borders, and to strengthen his brethren, that they may adorn the doctrine of God our Savior.[10]

It was inconceivable to Wesley that Christians would not forge a covenantal relationship with other Christians, because the very nature of Christianity was communal. He wrote:

By Christianity I mean that method of worshipping God which is here revealed to man by Jesus Christ. When I say this is essentially a social religion, I mean not only that it cannot subsist so well, but that it cannot subsist at all without society, without living and conversing with other men . . . To turn this religion into a solitary one is to destroy it.[11]

There are many reasons why Christianity is not a solitary religion. The first refers to the very nature of God. Christians understand God as a unity in community, a God in Three Persons, which means there is an essential fellowship within the Godhead revealed as Father, Son, and Spirit—or as some prefer, as Creator, Redeemer, and Sanctifier. God himself is not solitary! Furthermore, since creation, God the Father, Son, and Spirit are in relationship with that creation. The human person, created in God's image, is fundamentally a relational creature, created to be in relationship with other fellow creatures and with the Blessed Trinity. Wesley is absolutely correct in saying, "To turn this religion into a solitary one is to destroy it."

However, the church is necessary for salvation because the pursuit of, and possibility of, holiness can only be realized within the community of faith. In a preface to poetry written by himself and his brother Charles, John Wesley made clear this essential connection between holiness and the church:

> Solitary religion is not to be found [in the gospel of Christ]. "Holy solitaries" is a phrase no more consistent with the gospel than holy adulterers. The gospel of Christ knows of no religion but social; no holiness but social holiness. "Faith working by love" is the length and breadth and depth and height of Christian perfection. "This commandment have we from Christ, that he who loves God, love his brother also;" and that we manifest our love "by doing good unto all men; especially to them that are of the household of faith."[12]

In addition to the church expressing the very nature of God, the church is practically and functionally necessary as well, as indicated by the commitment required by Nazarenes when joining the church. Participation in the life of the church is necessary for salvation, because it is through faithfulness to the church as a means of grace and faithfulness to the means of grace within the church that the life of Christ is sustained and holiness is perfected. As Greathouse and Lyons write, "One cannot be holy alone. Holiness is experienced only within the context of a holy church, more specifically a particular local community of believers."[13]

The necessity of the church for salvation has not been widely recognized in American evangelicalism. The church is often seen as nonessential to the individual relationship with Jesus Christ. Participation in the life of the church may be understood as helpful and important, but unnecessary—in spite of the clear teaching of the New Testament that indicates otherwise.

When conducting membership classes in my church, I am often pressed to illustrate the necessity of the church for salvation and explain to prospective members what "means of grace" meant. When teaching the freshman college course Christian Formation, I have to do the same explaining for the same reason. In truth, it isn't difficult and most, regardless of previous presuppositions, recognize the need for church and quickly understand the means of grace. To help prospective members and college students understand the significance of the means of grace, I simply asked some leading questions. "Did you come to Christ through the church?" The testimony is almost always unanimously "Yes." More particularly, I asked, "How many of you came to faith through the preaching or teaching of the Word?" It is remarkable how many pointed to a particular message that was instrumental to their conversion.

To illustrate the necessity of the church for sustaining the Christian life, I ask, "How many Sundays can you miss church before it starts adversely affecting your relationship to Jesus Christ?" Obviously, that is impossible to quantify, but the various answers indicated they understood the point of the question. For the most devout, they confess they can't miss once! The other questions include, "How many of you are continuing to grow in grace as a consequence of praying and reading your Bible (which is the book of the community)?" "How many have been drawn closer to Christ through the receiving of the Lord's Supper?" and "Has anyone come to know the character of God better through active participation in the mission of the church?"

The necessity of the church as a means of grace to accomplish the work of God in their lives was revealed to prospective members and these young people through this little exercise. They easily recognized that the church and "faithful attendance upon the means of grace" were absolutely necessary for growth in grace, and they also recognized that the greater the faithfulness, the more likely the growth.

After illustrating the term and idea, I define them. "Means of grace" simply identifies the many different ways God's grace, in all of its manifestations, is communicated to God's people. The church can be referred to as a "means of grace." However, the phrase is usually understood as practices through which people are brought into the presence of God, through which God comes to them, and through which the Holy Spirit of God is sustained and nurtured in the life of the believer. Wesley defined them this way:

> By "means of grace" I understand outward signs, words, or actions, ordained of God, and appointed for this end, to be the ordinary channels whereby he might convey to men, preventing, justifying, or sanctifying grace. I use this expression, means of grace, because I know none better.[14]

Wesley identified three practices in his sermon "The Means of Grace," which the apostle Luke mentioned in his description of the early church at the beginning of the book of Acts. Luke reported that "they devoted themselves to the apostles' teaching and to the fellowship, to the breaking of bread and to prayer" (Acts 2:42). "Prayer," "searching the scriptures," and "receiving the Lord's Supper" were the three works of piety that were absolutely necessary for growth in Christlikeness, according to John Wesley.

The first work of piety was prayer, and its necessity can be illustrated with the life of Christ. Contemporary perceptions of Jesus' life do not often include Jesus spending much time alone in prayer, but even a cursory review of the gospel record indicates that he could be considered as much a monastic as a social worker. From just the gospel of Luke, we learn that Jesus was a man of prayer. It was as Jesus was praying that the Holy Spirit descended on him in the form of a dove at his baptism (Luke 3:21-22). Jesus spent the entire night in prayer before calling the twelve apostles (6:12-13). He had been in prayer when he asked the disciples who the crowds believed him to be (9:18-20). It was during prayer that Jesus was transfigured (vv. 28-31). It was Jesus praying that prompted the disciples asking him to teach them to pray (11:1). Jesus was at the Mount of Olives in prayer the night before he was crucified, because it was his usual place of prayer (22:39-42). Indeed, early on in his gospel, Luke reports that in spite of the large crowds of people who needed him, "Jesus often withdrew to lonely places and prayed" (5:16).

Luke frequently reported that the early church was prayerful. Following Jesus' ascension, as he had instructed, the disciples retreated to a house where they *all joined together constantly in prayer* (Acts 1:14a, emphasis added) and devoted themselves to prayer (2:42). Peter and John were at the temple and able to heal the man crippled from birth because it was the time of prayer—they had gone there to pray (3:1-2)! Upon being released from prison for healing that man, the first thing they did was return to the church to pray (4:23-24). The early church chose leaders to tend to the widows so that the Twelve could give their attention to prayer (6:4). Paul and Silas met Lydia in Thyatira because they were looking for a place to pray (16:13-14).

As might be expected, the apostle Paul was consistent in his instruction concerning prayer. To the church at Rome, he wrote: "Be joyful in hope, patient in affliction, *faithful in prayer*" (Romans 12:12, emphasis added). To the churches of Ephesus, he wrote: "And *pray in the Spirit* on all occasions with all kinds of prayers and requests. With this in mind, be alert and *always keep on praying* for all the saints" (Ephesians 6:18, emphasis added). To the church at Philippi: "Do not be anxious about anything, but in everything, by *prayer and petition, with thanksgiving, present your requests to God*" (Philippians 4:6, emphasis added). To the church at Colosse: "*Devote yourselves to prayer,* being watchful and thankful" (Colossians 4:2, emphasis added). And immediately before praying that the Thessalonians be entirely sanctified, he instructed them to "be joyful always; *pray continually*; give thanks in all circumstances, for this is God's will for you" (1 Thessalonians 5:16-18).

Prayer is so important for God's continued sanctifying work that when John Wesley was asked why Christians were not more holy, he replied, "Prayer especially is wanting."[15]

The second work of piety was "searching the scriptures." The sanctifying and sustaining power of hearing and reading the Word cannot be overestimated. The apostle Paul encouraged Timothy to faithfulness to the reading of the Scriptures:

But as for you, continue in what you have learned and have become convinced of, because you know those from whom you learned it, and how from infancy you have known the holy Scriptures, which are able to make you wise for salvation through faith in Christ Jesus. All Scripture is God-breathed and is useful for teaching, rebuking, correcting and training in righteousness, so that the man of God may be thoroughly equipped for every good work. (2 Timothy 3:14-17)

I discovered for myself the formative power of publicly reading scripture when I was a pastor. At the same time I began preaching from the lectionary, I incorporated into the worship service the public reading of Scripture. We began the service with a responsive reading of the assigned psalm. We prepared our hearts for the offering by reading either from one of the New Testament letters or from the Old Testament passage, and we prepared our hearts for prayer by reading from one of the Gospels. The service was designed around the suggested lectionary texts, and I allowed the written word to speak for itself without commentary. Thus, we heard Christ's teaching about subjects I was reluctant to broach. We heard God's judgment of sin, which I have already confessed that I neglected. We heard Jesus' descriptions of the kingdom of God. We heard Paul's pastoral counsel to people with grievances against one another. We listened together as Peter reminded us that we were a "peculiar" people and called to be holy. And it is the testimony of that local church that we became more reflective of the character of Christ as a direct consequence of listening together to the written Word of God. As a matter of historical fact, the biblical texts were originally written to be publicly read and corporately heard, not used primarily for personal devotion.

In addition to prayer and the searching of scriptures, Wesley was particularly concerned that his Methodists not neglect the third work of piety—faithfulness to the Lord's Supper. He understood the Lord's Supper to be an important "channel" of God's grace in the way that John Calvin did. There was a real spiritual presence of Christ attending the outward sign of bread and wine. According to Wesley, the Lord's Supper was not simply an effective way to remember what Christ had done on the cross; it was an occasion of Christ coming to his people and actually imparting power and grace through his spiritual presence. In a sermon written exclusively to encourage faithfulness to the Lord's Table, Wesley wrote:

> A second reason why every Christian should do this as often as he can, is, because the benefits of doing it are so great to all that do it in obedience to him; viz., the forgiveness of our past sins and the present strengthening and refreshing of our souls . . . As our bodies are strengthened by bread and wine, so are our souls by these tokens of the body and blood of Christ. This is the food of our souls: This gives strength to perform our duty, and leads us on to perfection. If, therefore, we have any regard for the plain command of Christ, if we desire the pardon of our sins, if we wish for strength to believe, to love and obey God, then we should neglect no opportunity of receiving the Lord's Supper; then we must never turn our backs on the feast which our Lord has prepared for us.[16]

In addition to these three works of piety, "works of mercy" serve as channels of God's grace. This includes feeding the hungry, clothing the naked, entertaining the stranger, and visiting those in prison or who are sick (see Matthew 25). Wesley considered these so crucial; he counseled that if one had a choice between a "work of piety" or a "work of mercy," the "work of mercy" should take precedence!

> Thus should he show his zeal for works of piety; but much more for works of mercy; seeing "God will have mercy and not sacrifice"—that is, rather than sacrifice. Whenever, therefore, one interferes with the other, works of mercy are to be preferred. Even reading, hearing, and prayer are to be omitted, or to be postponed, "at charity's almighty call"—when we are called to relieve the distress of our neighbor, whether in body or soul.[17]

Regardless of differing interpretations concerning particular means of grace, the necessity of "means" for the impartation of God's grace is broadly recognized. The life of the Holy Spirit is nurtured and sustained by faithfulness to these very ordinary practices—practices that have been a part of the church from the very beginning. Corporate worship, prayer, Bible study, fasting, "giving of our means," faithfulness to the sacraments, participation in ministry, and works of mercy, are, to name just a few, all conduits of God's grace. They are not disciplines as much as they are supplications. The life of God is sustained in us because God—as the Holy Spirit through Jesus Christ—comes to us when we faithfully attend to the means of grace.

Holiness, which is nothing other than the imparted character of Christ, is impossible if these means are neglected. Wesley was once asked how one should pursue holiness or Christlikeness; in an answer as relevant today as it was then, he replied:

> Not in careless indifference, or indolent inactivity; but in vigorous, universal obedience, in a zealous keeping of all the commandments, in watchfulness and painfulness, in denying ourselves, and taking up our cross daily; as well as in earnest prayer and fasting, and a close attendance on all the ordinances of God. And if any man dream of attaining it any other way, (yes, or of keeping it when it is attained, when he has received it even in the largest measure,) he deceives his own soul. It is true, we receive it by simple faith: But God does not, will not, give that faith, unless we seek it with all diligence, in the way which he hath ordained. This consideration may satisfy those who inquire, why so few have received the blessing. Inquire, how many are seeking it in this way; and you have a sufficient answer.[18]

Ask how many are seeking Christlikeness in this way, and you will have your answer as to why more are not.

In the very first chapter of this book, I suggested that one of the reasons today's holiness movement is anemic is because we have not considered the character of a holy God who hates sin and must destroy it for love's sake.

In the second and third chapters, I suggested that the reason for an anemic holiness movement is due to our reluctance to honestly acknowledge our own sinfulness and confess our inability to escape sin apart from God's grace.

In the fourth and fifth chapters, I suggested that a revitalized call to holiness requires recognizing that salvation has been provided by Jesus Christ through his atoning blood, and that salvation—from beginning to end—is all gift. Salvation is from grace to grace.

In the sixth and seventh chapters, I suggested that returning to an appreciation of the transformative nature of justifying grace—through the continuous presence of the Holy Spirit—would keep us from defining holiness legalistically, or believing it impossible altogether. Recognizing the life of Christ in us by virtue of the gift of the Holy Spirit points to the source and character of our holiness. It is Christ's righteousness within.

In the eighth chapter, I suggested that complete and continual consecration to God as a response to his gift of full salvation is critical to the life of holiness and is decisively sanctifying.

And in this chapter, I suggest that a revitalized call to holiness must be accompanied by a renewed appreciation for how God imparts that righteousness. God continues to give the holiness he expects of us through very ordinary, incarnational means of grace. The answer to the way forward can be found in the one-hundred-year-old membership ritual used in thousands of Nazarene churches around the world. By committing ourselves to the fellowship and mission of the church, and by endeavoring in every way to glorify God; by a humble walk, godly conversation, and holy service; by devotedly giving of our means; by faithful attendance to all the means of grace and by abstaining from all evil—by this, we will be well on the way to perfecting holiness of heart and life in the fear of the Lord.

11

CIRCUMCISION OF THE HEART

"I wonder at His great humility and my smallness—nothingness—I believe this is
where Jesus & I meet.—He is everything to me—and I—His own little one.
—so helpless—so empty—so small" (Mother Teresa).[1]

═══════════════ ◆ ═══════════════

A true saint of the church passed away on July 1, 2009. She was eighty-
three years old and her name was Mary Rose Gardner. Very few have ever
heard of her, and her death went unnoticed by all except her family, her
church, and her few remaining living friends. She was unremarkable by contemporary assessments. She never wrote a book. She was never on televi-
sion. She didn't receive any notable awards. She didn't break any athletic
records. She was the wife of a World War II veteran and the mother of two
daughters and a son. When she worked outside the home, it was as a man-
ager of the fabric department at the local K-Mart.

I was her pastor for over twenty years, and it was my privilege to watch
her live out a life of grace. She was faithful to Christ and her church in every
way possible. In Wesleyan terminology, she was faithful to the means of
grace. In holiness language, she attended church every time the doors were
open. She sat in the third row from the front, on the left side of the sanctuary Sunday morning and Sunday night. She gave when the offering plate was
passed and was as generous with her finances as possible, often giving more
than others thought she could afford. Every week, she hosted a small-group
Bible study in her home. Evidence of her sanctity was also found outside her
faithfulness to the church. Her conversations were always charitable. I personally cannot remember that she ever said an unkind word about anyone.
She was patient, kind, deferential, gentle, grateful, considerate, unpreten-
tious, and unpresuming. She had a sweet, self-deprecating sense of humor.

She had such a winsome, attractive disposition that everyone who knew her loved her; for they knew they could trust in her.

Her authentic, Christlike character was further revealed in her response to pain and sorrow. She was a picture of grace as she suffered from heart disease, which meant repeated and painful open-heart surgeries. Even in those times of need, she was deferential to the needs of others. She tenderly and patiently cared for her husband when he was dying of emphysema. And she quietly, albeit sorrowfully, came to terms with her life as a widow when he passed away. She insisted on living alone in a small two-bedroom duplex, not wanting to be a burden to her children, until she was no longer able to care for herself. Throughout the twenty years I knew her, she was a consistent model of sanctity for everyone in the church. On one occasion, I attempted to compliment her by repeating what I've written here about her. I said she was as Christlike as anyone I had ever known. Her response confirmed it. She said with alarm, and I quote, "Oh, pastor, if you only knew me."

In that seven-word response of Mary Rose Gardner is found a crucial characteristic of holiness. Those who are holy would be the last to recognize it.

Jesus describes this foundational attitude of those wholly transformed by God's grace in the first three beatitudes of the Sermon on the Mount. Jesus said that those who are a part of his kingdom are "poor in spirit," "mournful," and "meek." William Greathouse's understanding of Jesus' words is historically traditional:

> The first three describe the blessedness of those who discover their own spiritual poverty; who become painfully aware of their sin and the sin and suffering of the world; and who have committed themselves entirely to God as their defender in hope of the final triumph of the Kingdom.[2]

Perhaps the word "humble" can best describe this critical characteristic of holiness, in spite of the superficial way humility can be understood. Humility, properly understood, is what prompted Rose to her response and is nothing other than the honest recognition of absolute dependency on, and utter insufficiency apart from, the grace of God. Humility is simply consciousness of spiritual poverty that confesses need for God, and should, therefore, always be present in the life of the believer. As a matter of fact, the more one becomes like Christ, the more one becomes aware of dependency on him and insufficiency apart from him. Greathouse writes: "[The poor] are those who feel their spiritual poverty, who confess their moral bankruptcy before God."[3] In other words, the more like Christ we become, the more aware we become of how far from Christlikeness we are!

This is counterintuitive, and initially a little disconcerting, particularly among those who have been a part of the holiness tradition. It seems that there should be a growing self-awareness of Christlikeness the more like Christ one becomes. But the truth is immediately recognized by the quip, "I thought I met a holy man until he told me so himself!" And when I have asked pastors and students to imagine the response of the most Christlike person they know to the compliment I tried giving Rose Gardner, their answers are, without exception, variations of the answer I received: "Oh, pastor, if you only knew me."

Greathouse calls this fundamental characteristic of holiness the "paradox of perfection." In his biblical theology of holiness, *Wholeness in Christ,* Greathouse comments on Job in the second chapter of that book, writing that even though Job was blameless and upright, he was unaware of his righteousness. Greathouse writes:

> Nevertheless, when Job beheld God in His majestic holiness, his lips were silenced . . . The final proof of Job's perfection was the acknowledgment of his folly and shortcomings.[4]

The Bible shows evidence of this "paradox of perfection"; that is, those who are most Christlike are the very ones quickest to deny it. It is not insignificant that Jesus rebutted the attribution of "goodness" to himself when the rich young ruler came to ask Jesus what he must do to inherit eternal life. The apostle Luke records that this young man said, "Good teacher, what must I do to inherit eternal life?" Jesus' initial response is instructive: "'Why do you call me good?' Jesus answered. 'No one is good—except God alone'" (Luke 18:18-19). Jesus' insightful and convicting parable of the Pharisee and tax collector indicates the attitude of those God considers righteous. The parable begins with this clarifying comment: "To some who were confident of their own righteousness . . . Jesus told this parable" (v. 9). The one who was abject in the acknowledgment of his sinfulness was justified by God, and not the one who was conscious of his own faithful devotion. In this parable, Jesus told those self-righteous listeners that the one who was considered righteous by God was the one who could not even look up to heaven but only beat his breast and pray, "God, have mercy on me, a sinner" (v. 13). I have already mentioned the first three beatitudes found in Matthew's gospel, which describe the characteristic of those in the kingdom of heaven as those recognizing they have nothing to offer. When Jesus taught his disciples to pray in Matthew 6:11-12, he included a confession of dependence ("Give us today our daily bread") and a daily petition for forgiveness of sins ("Forgive us our debts, as we also have forgiven our debtors").

The apostle Paul was in full harmony with the teachings of Christ in this matter. In Romans, when he began his description of the attitudes and behaviors of those who offer themselves as living sacrifices, the very first quality he mentioned in that long list was humility:

> For by the grace given me I say to every one of you: Do not think of yourself more highly than you ought, but rather think of yourself with sober judgment, in accordance with the measure of faith God has given you. (Romans 12:3)

Just in case the Roman believers missed it, included in the other descriptions of the shared life of the sanctified are these imperatives: "Do not be proud . . . Do not be conceited" (v. 16). In this context, Paul is commanding the believers not to become proud of the gifts and graces they have received from God!

Perhaps the clearest evidence in Paul's letters for "humility" or "poverty of spirit" as a fundamental characteristic of the most holy can be found in the *kenosis* passage of the book of Philippians. Paul linked the nature of love to this confession of poverty:

> If you have any encouragement from being united with Christ, if any comfort from his love, if any fellowship with the Spirit, if any tenderness and compassion, then make my joy complete by being like-minded,

having the same love, being one in spirit and purpose. Do nothing out of selfish ambition or vain conceit, but in humility consider others better than yourselves. Each of you should look not only to your own interests, but also to the interests of others. Your attitude should be the same as that of Christ Jesus:

> Who, being in very nature God,
>
> did not consider equality with God something to be grasped,
>
> but made himself nothing,
>
> taking the very nature of a servant,
>
> being made in human likeness.
>
> And being found in appearance as a man,
>
> he humbled himself
>
> and became obedient to death—even death on a cross! (Philippians 2:1-8)

Paul's call for believers to empty themselves like Christ was not a pretentious or artificial humiliation. In this passage, Paul did not expect believers to pretend they were something they were not, as if they could feign humility. This attitude or spirit or mind that is expected of followers of Christ should be the same as Christ's as he hung on the cross; impoverished, destitute, absolutely dependent, and trusting exclusively in God's vindication. Indeed, if this was the mind or attitude of every believer, it would make Paul's commands easily fulfilled. Of course believers would consider others better than themselves—how could they not, if they had the mind of Christ revealed most fully on the cross?

A couple of paragraphs later in that same letter to Philippi, Paul testified that he intentionally rejected knowledge of his own righteousness for the sake of righteousness from Christ that was, by nature, all gift:

> But whatever was to my profit I now consider loss for the sake of Christ. What is more, I consider everything a loss compared to the surpassing greatness of knowing Christ Jesus my Lord, for whose sake I have lost all things. I consider them rubbish, that I may gain Christ and be found in him, not having a righteousness of my own that comes from the law,

but that which is through faith in Christ—the righteousness that comes from God and is by faith. (3:7-9)

Paul understood himself as absolutely dependent on, and utterly deficient apart from, Christ. This is discerned from what he wrote immediately following his confession:

Not that I have already obtained all this, or have already been made perfect, but I press on to take hold of that for which Christ Jesus took hold of me. Brothers, I do not consider myself yet to have taken hold of it. But one thing I do: Forgetting what is behind and straining toward what is ahead, I press on toward the goal to win the prize for which God has called me heavenward in Christ Jesus. (Vv. 12-14)

The church's long-held tradition recognizes the essential place such humility holds in holiness. Macarius, a fourth-century Syrian monastic, whose sermons John Wesley loved and recommended, described those who were serious about the pursuit of holiness:

The more they perceive themselves advancing in spiritual perfection, the more do they hunger and thirst for a greater share of and increase in grace. And the richer they become spiritually, the poorer they consider themselves . . . The person who truly loves God and Christ, even though he may perform a thousand good works, considers himself as having done nothing because of his insatiable longing for the Lord . . . Such a one regards himself as the greatest of all sinners. He carries this thought ever with him as a part of his very makeup. And the more he progresses in knowledge of God, the more simple and unlearned he considers himself . . . This grace [of humility] acts as a guiding force, almost second nature to him . . . It feeds the mind and lifts it up to Heaven, to the perfect world, to everlasting rest.[5]

John Wesley recommended Thomas á Kempis's manual for spiritual growth as the first book Wesley's followers should read after the Bible. Thomas á Kempis wrote:

It is the humble man whom God protects and liberates; it is the humble whom He loves and consoles. To the humble He turns and upon them He bestows great grace . . . He reveals His secrets to the humble, and with kind invitation bids them come to Him . . . Moreover, if you will come to the height of perfection, do not think that you have advanced in virtue until you can feel humbly in your heart that you have less humility and less virtue than anyone else.[6]

It shouldn't be surprising, then, that Wesley understood this "paradox of perfection." In the sermon "Circumcision of the Heart," which was drawn from Romans 2:29, Wesley described those he considered having been cleansed from sin, "filled with all the virtues of Christ" and "perfect even as God the Father is perfect." The first attribute, upon which faith, hope, and love depended, was humility:

> Humility, a right judgment of ourselves, cleanses our minds from those high conceits of our own perfection, from that undue opinion of our own abilities and attainments, which are the genuine fruit of a corrupted nature . . . [Humility] convinces us that we are by nature wretched, and poor, and miserable, and blind, and naked. It convinces us, that in our best estate we are, of ourselves, all sin and vanity . . . that there is no whole part in our soul, that all the foundations of our nature are out of course.
>
> At the same time we are convinced, that we are not sufficient of ourselves to help ourselves; that, without the Spirit of God, we can do nothing but add sin to sin; that it is He alone who works in us by his almighty power, either to will or do that which is good; it being as impossible for us even to think a good thought, without the supernatural assistance of his Spirit, as to create ourselves, or to renew our whole souls in righteousness and true holiness.[7]

It must be remembered that Wesley was not describing the attitude needed for the possibility of holiness, so that once one was cleansed from sin, one no longer needed to consider himself or herself this way. Wesley was describing the attitude of one already made perfect and, in his words, "endued with those virtues which were also in Christ Jesus." The attitude of humility that recognizes one's own poverty was Christ's attitude. Wesley wrote: "This is that lowliness of mind, which they have learned of Christ, who follow his example and tread in his steps."

Obviously, humility is not the only characteristic of those who are like Christ, but this attitude of absolute dependence and recognition of deficiency leads to all the other perfections. Humility inevitably necessitates faith, since trusting in Christ for salvation is the only recourse to those conscious of their poverty. Faith results in grateful love for God, who would, in Christ, condescend to save such helpless and even obstinate creatures. As the apostle John wrote, "We love because he first loved us" (1 John 4:19). This love for him manifests itself as a Christlike love for others, since God has provided the definition of love in the gracious self-denying sacrifice of Christ. Love finally encompasses all the other qualities associated with Christlikeness. Paul states that love is the defining character of holiness in several places in his letters, most notably in 1 Corinthians 13, but also in Romans. According to Paul, when we offer ourselves as a living sacrifice—which is the "reasonable" response to what God has done for us—our relationships with each other will be one of love in all its various expressions. Paul writes:

> Let no debt remain outstanding, except the continuing debt to love one another, for he who loves his fellowman has fulfilled the law. The commandments, "Do not commit adultery," "Do not murder," "Do not steal," "Do not covet," and whatever other commandment there may be, are summed up in this one rule: "Love your neighbor as yourself." Love does no harm to its neighbor. Therefore love is the fulfillment of the law. (Romans 13:8-10)

This is what John Wesley understood. In his sermon "On Perfection" he explained of what holiness consisted:

> It is the "loving the Lord his God with all his heart, and with all his soul and with all his mind." This is the sum of Christian perfection: It is all comprised in that one word, Love. The first branch of it is the love of God: And as he that loves God loves his brother also, it is inseparably connected with the second: "Thou shall love thy neighbor as thyself . . ." "On these two commandments hang all the Law and the Prophets."[8]

Thus, humility—the truthful recognition of one's own inherent poverty, deficiency, and absolute dependence on the grace of God—results in the fulfillment of the law of love! Those living out the incarnate life of Christlike love are most conscious that they are, in and of themselves, "wretched, and poor, and miserable, and blind, and naked." In other words, it is thoroughly in keeping with the essence of holiness to state that the most holy would be the last to recognize it. As Rose Gardner said, "Oh, pastor, if you only knew me."

This humility does not prevent believers from recognizing God's work in their lives in specific ways. Christians being sanctified are able to recognize how God's grace has been particularly transforming. Paul identifies specific qualities as evidence of the life of God in the sanctified believer. The evidence, or fruit of the Holy Spirit, is "love, joy, peace, patience, kindness, goodness, faithfulness, gentleness and self-control" (Galatians 5:22-23a). Thus, holy humility, in which a believer continues to recognize his or her dependence and deficiency, does not mean blindness to the effective work of God in his or her life. It simply means that he or she always knows from whom this Christlikeness is derived. The believer is becoming more and more aware of just how full and rich is the holiness of Christ, and how far he or she has yet to go to perfectly realize it.

This humility, which keeps before us our poverty—does not call into question that holiness is possible, either. The idea that the most holy would be the last to recognize it might be a little disconcerting to those taught to profess having been made holy. In years past, the holiness tradition encouraged those who had experienced the grace of being entirely sanctified to testify to it. This encouragement was motivated, in part, by the desire to affirm that holiness was possible. With the emphasis on the necessity of holiness, the crisis experience of entire sanctification became primary evidence of its reality.

To that end, testifying to the experience of entire sanctification was critically assuring. The call to holiness, without which "no one will see the Lord" (Hebrews 12:14) was such a prominent proclamation in the holiness tradition that not having experienced entire sanctification called into question a believer's entire salvation. Consecrating oneself for entire sanctification, therefore, also provided much-needed assurance of salvation. In the holiness tradition, entire consecration was certainly sanctifying, but also, and arguably as important, graciously assuring. Thus, it's understandable why some find disconcerting the suggestion that the most holy would be the last to recognize it, for this seems to call into question the possibility of holiness and also the assurance of it.

However, the evidence of sanctity ought not to be found simply in personal claims of someone who has been sanctified. The evidence of holiness is found in the character and spirit of those who exemplify the spirit of Christ, which includes the Christlike spirit of humility, a humility that precludes the most holy from recognizing it. Salvation's assurance should not be found in recollecting a particular experience, or even our assessment of how God is presently sanctifying—as important and assuring as these might be. Assurance of salvation should be found in the Christ who gave his life for ours.

The holiness tradition might have been helped by Wesley's wise counsel. He was asked if those who had experienced the grace of entire sanctification should testify to it. Wesley acknowledged that one who had been entirely sanctified would find it difficult not to speak of it, that there were indeed appropriate occasions that could call for such a testimony. But he cautioned against testifying to this grace indiscriminately. In *A Plain Account of Christian Perfection,* he wrote:

> It would be advisable not to speak of it to them that know not God; (it is most likely, it would only provoke them to contradict and blaspheme;) nor to others, without some particular reason, without some good in view. And then he should have special care to avoid all appearance of boasting; to speak with the deepest humility and reverence, giving all the glory to God.[9]

Humility would not necessarily preclude someone from speaking of this work of God in his or her life. It would simply mandate the nature of that testimony. Testifying to this work of God would take on the character of the apostle Paul's testimony: "Not that I have already obtained all this, or have already been made perfect, but I press on to take hold of that for which Christ Jesus took hold of me" (Philippians 3:12).

John Wesley wrote that those who are most Christlike are those most conscious of their need for and dependence on Christ: "None feels their need of Christ like these; none so entirely depend upon him." According to

Wesley, the more like Christ one becomes, the more one becomes aware of how far from Christlike they are—conversely, those who are least Christlike might be the most likely to affirm it! Again, this doesn't deny the possibility of holiness. It just means that the ones who are holy would be the last to know! As a true saint of the church said to my suggestion that she was, indeed, a saint, "Oh, pastor, if you only knew me." As I wrote above, that response confirmed it.

SECTION FOUR

HOPE

12

THE WAY TO THE KINGDOM

"It is not we who go to heaven, it is heaven that comes to earth" (N. T. Wright).[1]

◆

In August of 2002, Belleville First Church of the Nazarene presented my wife and me with a generous travel voucher in recognition of twenty years of ministry to the congregation. They said that we could go wherever we wanted, whenever we wanted, for however long we wanted! It was an extravagant act of kindness for which we will always be grateful.

We immediately decided that we would go to Europe, as that had been one of our unspoken dreams for as long as we could remember. We decided to go the following summer, which would give us about ten months to plan and prepare for a once-in-a-lifetime trip. For the next ten months, that is what we did. We planned and prepared. We researched what was reasonable to see in three weeks. We talked to everyone we knew who had been to Europe to learn where we should go. We bought travel books for each of the countries we wanted to visit and read them thoroughly. We rented travel videos and watched travel shows on cable. We memorized important phrases in French, German, and Italian. After we had settled on a rather ambitious itinerary, we bought the airline tickets, reserved two rental cars (one for England and one for the continent), and bought two round-trip tickets on the ferry across the English Channel. We researched hotels, made those reservations, and printed out pictures of them so we would recognize them when we arrived. We purchased all the tickets to all the museums we wanted to see on the days we wanted to visit. We printed all the maps we would need, with driving distances indicated and travel times estimated. We put all this information in a large notebook, with each day's itinerary clearly marked, so that when we got to Europe, all we would have to do is follow the explicit directions we had meticulously provided ourselves!

About a week before we left, my father and I were talking about the much-anticipated trip and he said, tongue in cheek, that he wasn't even sure why we were still going. He thought that with all the detailed preparations we had made, there really wasn't much point in actually going since we virtually had been living in Europe all year long. So he suggested that we ought to save the money and not go, since it was as if we had already been there.

Of course, he was teasing. But there was a profound element of truth in what he said. When we did actually make the trip, it was obviously more fulfilling to actually walk the streets and see the sights than to just look at pictures, as we had been doing all year. Once we were there, we recognized everything we had hoped to see. It wasn't completely foreign. It all looked very familiar. As it turned out, the actual trip to Europe—which we had been anticipating for almost a year—had overflowed into our lives before we had ever left the United States. That future trip had colored and conditioned that entire year. While we certainly had never been to Europe, those preparations were so thorough that it was almost as if we had already been there.

The anticipation of that future event, which colored and conditioned that entire previous year, applies to the Christian life in general and has important implications for a doctrine of holiness in particular. The gospel is not only about what God has done in the past; it is not only about what God is doing in the present; but it is also about what God is going to do in the future. While the redemptive work of God was completed in the life, death, and resurrection of Jesus Christ, it has not yet been brought to complete fulfillment. There is more. While it is certainly right and important for Christians to celebrate what God has done in the past, and while it is certainly right and appropriate for Christians to celebrate what God is doing in the present, the celebration is incomplete if it doesn't include joyful anticipation of what God has promised to do in the future. The worship of Christ is not only remembrance but also anticipation. As the liturgy says, "Christ has died, Christ is risen, Christ will come again!"

I began this book with a call for Christians to look forward. In the first chapter, I pled for serious consideration of God's promised judgment on sin and evil. This is how the apostle Paul began his formal argument in his letter to the church of Rome, and as I mentioned in the introduction, this is how I also began. In that first chapter, I mentioned that I was many years into my pastoral ministry before I preached a message devoted exclusively to the promised return of Christ and his subsequent judgment. It was a misguided attempt to make the gospel more appealing; however, I was omitting more than I intended. While I was "protecting" my church from the uncomfortable truths of God's wrath and Christ's judgment, I was conversely denying them the assurance of that glorious future—the future that ought to have been impacting their present. I realized that if I didn't preach about hell, I didn't preach much about heaven, either! If I didn't preach about the sentence of death on evil, I didn't preach about the promise of the new creation! I intended to preach salvation, confined to God's past redemptive acts, and how those past events impacted the present. But by default, salvation excluded God's future redemptive acts and therefore, the promise of that future salvation was made largely irrelevant to the present. In other words, I preached much about humility, faith, and love, but I did not preach much about hope. One of the unintended consequences of neglecting to preach on the hope for the future was that the promise of holiness was compromised.

The apostle Paul certainly didn't neglect writing about what the future held for God's people. He certainly didn't neglect writing about the appropriateness of allowing that promised future to orient, condition, or affect the present. Hope, and its very real impact on the present, was not a minor theme in Paul's letters (nor is it a minor theme in any of the other writings of the Bible!). He certainly thought it appropriate for that promised future to motivate believers to Christlikeness.

In the concluding paragraphs of his letter to the church of Rome, after writing that love was the most reasonable response to the extravagant mercy of God, he provided incentive to fulfill the debt of love by referencing the future coming of Christ:

> And do this [love], understanding the present time. The hour has come for you to wake up from your slumber, because our salvation is nearer now than when we first believed. The night is nearly over; the day is almost here. (Romans 13:11-12a)

The salvation in this passage refers to both the deliverance from God's wrath and the future fulfillment of salvation. Greathouse's and Lyons' comments on these verses are helpful:

Salvation refers, negatively, to the final rescue of believers from God's wrath at the time of the Judgment (Rom 2:5, 8, 9; 5:9, see Gal 1:4; 1 Thess 1:10; 5:8-9). Positively, it means full entrance into all the blessings in store for the eschatological people of God—"the glory that will be revealed in us" (Rom 8:18), "the redemption of our bodies" (v 23), "glory, honor and immortality . . . eternal life" (2:7).[2]

Paul believed that knowledge of the imminent coming of Christ ought to motivate believers to holiness; immediately following his assertion that the night was nearly over, he wrote:

So let us put aside the deeds of darkness and put on the armor of light. Let us behave decently, as in the daytime, not in orgies and drunkenness, not in sexual immorality and debauchery, not in dissension and jealousy. Rather, clothe yourselves with the Lord Jesus Christ, and do not think about how to gratify the desires of the sinful nature. (Romans 13:12b-14)

As Greathouse and Lyons noted, Paul repeatedly calls on the Christians in Rome to consider the promised future, and one of the reasons was for its motivational potential. He was not reluctant to use the future judgment with its rewards and punishments as a spur to holiness:

God "will give to each person according to what he has done." To those who by persistence in doing good seek glory, honor and immortality, he will give eternal life. But for those who are self-seeking and who reject the truth and follow evil, there will be wrath and anger. There will be trouble and distress for every human being who does evil: first for the Jew, then for the Gentile; but glory, honor and peace for everyone who does good: first for the Jew, then for the Gentile. For God does not show favoritism. (Romans 2:6-11)

This passage provides incentive for rejecting sin and pursuing holiness. Serious consideration of final judgment was evidently quite appropriate, if the number of times the apostle Paul refers to it in his other correspondence is any indication.

For example, in the letter to the church of Corinth, Paul testifies that the knowledge of God's future promises motivated him:

So we make it our goal to please him, whether we are at home in the body or away from it. For we must all appear before the judgment seat of Christ, that each one may receive what is due him for the things done while in the body, whether good or bad. Since, then, we know what it is to fear the Lord, we try to persuade men. (2 Corinthians 5:9-11a)

In his letter to the church at Philippi, he testifies to the motivating power of hope for God's future:

But one thing I do: Forgetting what is behind and straining toward what is ahead, I press on toward the goal to win the prize for which God has called me heavenward in Christ Jesus. All of us who are mature should take such a view of things. (Philippians 3:13b-15a)

In one of Paul's first letters—written to comfort those confused about the timing of the coming of Christ—he used Christ's second coming to encourage believers to holiness in two different places:

May the Lord make your love increase and overflow for each other and for everyone else, just as ours does for you. May he strengthen your hearts so that you will be blameless and holy in the presence of our God and Father when our Lord Jesus comes with all his holy ones. (1 Thessalonians 3:12-13)

In the same letter, in a most familiar text to those in the holiness movement, Paul connects the call to being sanctified entirely with the second coming of Christ:

May God himself, the God of peace, sanctify you through and through. May your whole spirit, soul and body be kept blameless at the coming of our Lord Jesus Christ. The one who calls you is faithful and he will do it. (1 Thessalonians 5:23-24)

John Wesley understood the incentive to holiness provided by consideration of the future. When he preached before that congregation of magistrates, Wesley did not refrain from using the second coming as motivation to sanctity. After calling attention to the fact that those judges in that congregation were going to be judged themselves, he wrote:

> What manner of persons then ought we to be, in all holy conversation and godliness? We know it cannot be long before the Lord will descend with the voice of the archangel and the trumpet of God; when every one of us shall appear before him, and give account of his own works. "Wherefore, beloved, seeing you look for these things," seeing you know He will come and will not tarry, "be diligent, that you may be found of him in peace, without spot and blameless." Why should you not? Why should one of you be found on the left hand, at his appearing? He does not desire that any should perish, but that all should come to repentance; by repentance, to faith in a bleeding Lord; by faith, to spotless love, to the full image of God renewed in the heart, and producing all holiness of conversation. Can you doubt of this, when you remember, the Judge of all is likewise the Savior of all? Has he not bought you with his own blood, that you might not perish, but have everlasting life? O make proof of his mercy, rather than his justice; of his love, rather than the thunder of his power! He is not far from every one of us.[3]

Serious consideration of the final judgment—with its rewards and punishments—is evidently appropriate incentive for the pursuit of holiness. Anticipation of Christ's coming ought to spur believers to holiness and the general neglect of second-coming preaching might give one answer as to why the pursuit of holiness is not a more serious endeavor.

However, there is more to understanding about the nature of the Christian's hope than hope for escape from God's wrath, or hope for his reward. Confident hope in the future that God has promised should alter how believers understand and interpret their present situation. As important as hope is in providing an incentive to holiness, it does more. By virtue of hope, believers are enabled, or empowered, to live the life of holiness in the present age. Hope not only serves as the motivation but also helps make the holiness to which all are called a present possibility.

The power of hope to empower the believers toward holiness is illustrated in the profoundly important eighth chapter of Romans. In this passage, Paul wrote that all creation is groaning for full redemption, and he revealed the power of hope to effect the very change for which it was longing. This vision of future redemption, which is made real by the hope that God gives, enables believers to live in that future through that very hope. Paul wrote:

> I consider that our present sufferings are not worth comparing with the glory that will be revealed in us. The creation waits in eager expectation for the sons of God to be revealed. For the creation was subjected to frustration, not by its own choice, but by the will of the one who subjected it, in hope that the creation itself will be liberated from its bondage to decay and brought into the glorious freedom of the children of God. We know that the whole creation has been groaning as in the pains of childbirth right up to the present time. Not only so, but we ourselves, who have the firstfruits of the Spirit, groan inwardly as we wait eagerly for our adoption as sons, the redemption of our bodies. For in this hope we were saved. But hope that is seen is no hope at all. Who hopes for what he already has? But if we hope for what we do not yet have, we wait for it patiently. (Vv. 18-25)

According to the apostle Paul, believers are to have so much confidence in the future hope of the new creation that it conditions, colors, and even changes the present situation. The certainty of what God has promised—nothing less than the complete redemption of all of creation, which includes the physical body of the human creature—empowers the believer, in this particular example, to faithful patience. In other words, hope enables the suffering believer to see, not only the world as it is presently, but to see the world as it will be. Thus, the ability to be patient is a consequence of hope. The promise of the new creation allows for that new creation to begin today, even in the midst of its groaning! "Hope saves," or to state it as the apostle Paul does: "In this hope we were saved."

In a parallel passage, in the letter to the church at Corinth, Paul wrote that hope, by providing eternal perspective, impacts the present and changes it. In this passage, he was writing of the hardships that accompanied his ap-

ostolic ministry, and he identifies the crucial place of hope in the fulfillment
of that ministry:

> We know that the one who raised the Lord Jesus from the dead will also
> raise us with Jesus and present us with you in his presence. . . . There-
> fore we do not lose heart. Though outwardly we are wasting away, yet
> inwardly we are being renewed day by day. For our light and momentary
> troubles are achieving for us an eternal glory that far outweighs them all.
> So we fix our eyes not on what is seen, but on what is unseen. For what is
> seen is temporary, but what is unseen is eternal. (2 Corinthians 4:14, 16-18)

Confident hope in the promised future ought to change the very way
believers understand and interpret their present situation. Just as my wife and
I allowed the anticipation of that future trip to Europe to affect almost the entire previous year, the believer should allow the anticipation of what God has
promised to alter the present—so much so, that it is almost as if they were
already living in that future. Hope helps make the future a present reality.

The ability of hope in a promised future to effectively change the present is not simply a consequence of the eternal perspective that hope brings.
The most important reason believers are enabled to live hopefully—that is,
in the present world as if they were in the promised future—is because the
Holy Spirit has been given as a promissory note of that future. The gift of the
Holy Spirit, according to the apostle Paul, is proof that the future promises
of God will be realized. The Holy Spirit brings God's future into the present,
and because of the gift of the Holy Spirit, the present situation has actually
been changed. The new creation has begun, as the familiar words written
to the Corinthians indicate: "Therefore, if anyone is in Christ, he is a new
creation; the old has gone, the new has come!" (5:17).

The Holy Spirit as the present evidence of the future promise is made
clear in that crucial Romans 8 passage. Paul wrote that believers "have the
firstfruits of the Spirit" (v. 23). The intentional use of the word "firstfruits,"
which would have been very familiar to the Jewish people, indicates that
Paul understood that believers, inhabited by the Holy Spirit, were the present
and initial evidence of God's future and final redemption.

The Holy Spirit as a promissory note, guaranteeing the full redemption of all creation, is a recurrent theme in Paul's writings. In Romans 5 he indicates that the ultimate result of justifying grace by faith was greater hope for the fulfillment of God's purposes, precisely through the gift of the Holy Spirit:

Therefore, since we have been justified through faith, we have peace with God through our Lord Jesus Christ, through whom we have gained access by faith into this grace in which we now stand. And we rejoice in the hope of the glory of God. Not only so, but we also rejoice in our sufferings, because we know that suffering produces perseverance; perseverance, character; and character, hope. And hope does not disappoint us, because God has poured out his love into our hearts by the Holy Spirit, whom he has given us. (Vv. 1-5)

The Holy Spirit as the present evidence of God's promised future redemption is indicated in Paul's second letter to the church at Corinth:

Now it is God who makes both us and you stand firm in Christ. He anointed us, set his seal of ownership on us, and put his Spirit in our hearts as a deposit, guaranteeing what is to come. (1:21-22)

A few paragraphs later, he reiterated: "Now it is God who . . . has given us the Spirit as a deposit, guaranteeing what is to come" (5:5).

To the church at Ephesus, he wrote the same:

Having believed, you were marked in him with a seal, the promised Holy Spirit, who is a deposit guaranteeing our inheritance until the redemption of those who are God's possession—to the praise of his glory. (Ephesians 1:13*b*–14)

The significance of understanding the Holy Spirit—as the evidence of the future hope—to a doctrine of holiness is easily seen. God the Creator, through the redemptive work of Christ Jesus, and by the sanctifying work of the Holy Spirit, has brought the kingdom of heaven to earth in and among God's people. Believers, inhabited by God the Holy Spirit, have been incorporated into this new kingdom that is and is still to come. The Holy Spirit's presence is sanctifying precisely because it is the Holy Spirit who brings to fruition God's purposes in the present. The hope, therefore, which calls us forward to the final new creation is a hope grounded in the work of God in the past and in the present. Thus, hope is not simply wishful thinking. It is based in the sanctifying work of the Holy Spirit. The evidence of the promise of that future is the holiness exemplified in and among God's people. The call to holiness can be understood as nothing other than the call to live out the future redemption of God here and now. In short, holiness is the present evidence of the future kingdom of God.

This understanding of holiness as evidence of a promised future was an integral part of the holiness tradition in its earliest days. The emphasis on the baptism of the Holy Spirit among early Nazarenes correlated their understanding of the Holy Spirit as evidence of the future kingdom with their understanding of the Spirit as sanctifying.[4] The Holy Spirit was sanctifying precisely because the Holy Spirit was the down payment of the promised redemption of all creation. In short, heaven came to earth among God's people in the person of the Holy Spirit. Early Nazarenes sang about it in precisely this way; in a 1903 hymn written for the holiness movement—and which is still in the most recent Nazarene hymnal—they sang these words:

> We find many people who can't understand
>> Why we are so happy and free.
> We've crossed over Jordan to Canaan's fair land,
>> And this is like heaven to me.
>
> O this is like heaven to me,
> Yes this is like heaven to me.
> I've crossed over Jordan to Canaan's fair land,
> And this is like heaven to me.
>
> So when we are happy we sing and we shout.
>> Some don't understand us, I see.
> We're filled with the Spirit, there isn't a doubt.
>> And this is like heaven to me.[5]

This was entirely consistent with Wesley, for he also believed that the life of holiness would anticipate the joys of heaven. He described the fullness of salvation as both holiness and happiness:

This holiness and happiness, joined in one, are sometimes styled, in the inspired writings, "the kingdom of God," and sometimes, "the kingdom of heaven." It is termed "the kingdom of God," because it is the immediate fruit of God's reigning in the soul. So soon as ever he takes unto himself his mighty power, they are instantly filled with this "righteousness, and peace, and joy in the Holy Ghost." It is called "the kingdom of heaven," because it is (in a degree) heaven opened in the soul. For whosoever they are that experience this, they can [testify] before angels and men,

"Everlasting life is won,

Glory is on earth begun . . ."

And this "kingdom of God" or of heaven, "is at hand."[6]

Thus, we are brought full circle. I began this book by suggesting that one of the reasons for the apparent indifference to holiness among contemporary evangelicals was the lack of consideration given to the character of a holy God who hates sin and will destroy it in the coming kingdom, all for love's sake.

I am concluding by suggesting that the holiness tradition might be revitalized by recognizing the promissory nature of holiness. Holiness is not simply sought as a way to escape future condemnation, but is a way to realize the character of the kingdom of heaven here in this present world. Holiness is the evidence that the kingdom of heaven has begun!

To summarize, the holiness message is this: the kingdom of heaven has indeed begun among God's people everywhere and is characterized by honest recognition of our absolute dependence on God, unmitigated trust in Christ's provision, confidence in the indwelling Spirit of God to complete this work, and grateful, sacrificial service in response to salvation so freely granted.

To summarize even more succinctly, the holiness message is nothing other than this: the kingdom of heaven has begun and is characterized among God's people and in his church, by humility, faith, hope, and love.

NOTES

Page 9

1. John Wesley, *The Works of John Wesley,* 3rd ed., 14 vols. (Reprint, Kansas City: Beacon Hill Press of Kansas City, 1986), 5:12.

Chapter 1

1. Joseph Cardinal Ratzinger, *Introduction to Christianity* (San Francisco: Ignatius Press, 2004), 31.

2. H. Richard Niebuhr, *The Kingdom of God in America* (New York: Harper & Brothers, 1937), 193.

3. Wesley, *Works,* 6:65.

Chapter 2

1. *Sing to the Lord* (Kansas City: Lillenas Publishing Company, 1993), 85.

2. John Wesley, *Explanatory Notes on the Bible* (London: William Bowyer, 1755), 384.

3. *Church of the Nazarene Manual: 2005-2009* (Kansas City: Nazarene Publishing House, 2005), 37-38.

4. Richard John Neuhaus, *Freedom for Ministry* (Grand Rapids: Eerdmans, 1992), 94.

5. William M. Greathouse and George Lyons, *Romans 1-8: A Commentary in the Wesleyan Tradition* (Kansas City: Beacon Hill Press of Kansas City, 2008), 70.

6. Gustaf Aulen, *The Faith of the Christian Church* (Philadelphia: Muhlenberg Press, 1960), 117-18.

7. H. Orton Wiley, *Christian Theology,* Vol. I (Kansas City: Beacon Hill Press, 1940), 370, 385-86.

Chapter 3

1. Oswald Chambers, *My Utmost for His Highest* (New York: Dodd, Mead & Co, 1935), 169.

2. Reported in *The Times* of London online: March 10, 2008, http://www.timeson-line.co.uk/tol/comment/faith/article3517050.ece.

3. Wesley, *Works,* 5:158-61.

4. http://home.snu.edu/~hculbert/selfexam.htm.

5. Wesley, *Works,* 8:272-73.

6. Ibid., 273.

7. For example, see George Barna, *Boiling Point: Monitoring Cultural Shifts in the 21st Century* (Ventura, Calif.: Regal Books, 2001).

Chapter 4

1. Blaise Pascal, *Pensees* (New York: Penguin Books, 1966), 65.

2. Thomas Oden, *John Wesley's Scriptural Christianity* (Grand Rapids: Zondervan Publishing House, 1994), 157.

3. Wesley, *Works,* 6:63.

4. Philip Schaff, ed., *The Creeds of Christendom,* Vol. III (Grand Rapids: Baker Books, 1996), 808-9.

5. http://www.lcms.org/pages/internal.asp?NavID=566. (Site now discontinued.)

6. Schaff, *Creeds of Christendom,* 615.

7. *Nazarene Manual: 2005-2009,* 31-32.

8. G. K. Chesterton, *Orthodoxy* (San Francisco: Ignatius Press, 1995), 19.

9. Augustine, *Confessions* (New York: Penguin Books, 1981), 47-48.

10. Wesley, *Works,* 6:65.

Chapter 5

1. Quoted in Gustaf Aulen, *Christus Victor* (Eugene, Ore.: Wipf & Stock, 2003), 34.

2. Wesley, *Works,* 13:34.

3. Alister E. McGrath, *The Christian Theology Reader* (Oxford: Blackwell Publishing, 2007), 358-59.

4. *Sing to the Lord,* 225.

5. Aulen, *Christus Victor,* 58.

6. Alister E. McGrath, *Christianity: An Introduction,* 2nd ed. (Malden, Mass.: Blackwell Publishing, 2006), 147.

7. Greathouse and Lyons, *Romans 1-8,* 129.

8. Wesley, *Works,* 5:239.

9. Ibid., 235.

10. Ibid., 239.

11. N. T. Wright, *The Crown and the Fire: Meditations on the Cross and the Life of the Spirit* (Grand Rapids: Eerdmans, 1997), 44.

12. Quoted in Tom Wright, *Small Faith—Great God: Biblical Faith for Today's Christians* (Old Tappan, N.J.: Fleming H. Revell, 1978), 49-50.

13. Ted M. Dorman, *A Faith for All Seasons* (Nashville: Broadman & Holman, 2001), 181.

14. Wesley, *Works,* 5:57.

15. *Sing to the Lord,* 432.

Chapter 6

1. John Dillenberger, ed., *Martin Luther: Selections from His Writings* (Garden City, N.Y.: Anchor Books, 1961), 11.

2. Wesley, *Works,* 1:95.

3. Ibid., 103.

4. Greathouse and Lyons, *Romans 1-8,* 138.

5. *The Book of Discipline of the United Methodist Church* (Nashville: United Methodist Publishing House, 1996), 59.

6. Schaff, *Creeds of Christendom,* 10.

7. *Nazarene Manual: 2005-2009,* 34.

8. Greathouse and Lyons, *Romans 1-8,* 139.

9. Wesley, *Works,* 6:49.

10. Kenneth J. Collins, *The Theology of John Wesley* (Nashville: Abingdon Press, 2007), 196.

11. *Book of Discipline of the United Methodist Church,* 63.

12. *Nazarene Manual: 2005-2009,* 34-35.

13. *Sing to the Lord,* 343.

14. Wesley, *Works,* 5:63.

Chapter 7

1. Quoted in F. F. Bruce, *The Epistle to the Hebrews,* rev. ed. (Grand Rapids: Eerdmans, 1990), 138.

2. Wesley, *Works,* 8:285.

3. Ibid., 3:212.

4. Ibid., 5:63.

5. Ibid., 10:366.

6. Ibid., 6:45.

7. Greathouse and Lyons, *Romans 1-8,* 174.

8. Wesley, *Works,* 5:146-47.

Chapter 8

1. Wesley, *Works,* 8:49.

2. Ibid.

3. Ibid., 104.

4. Ibid., 49.

5. Ibid., 10:82.

6. Theodore G. Tappert, ed., *The Book of Concord* (Philadelphia: Fortress Press, 1959), 415.

7. Schaff, *Creeds of Christendom,* 629-30.

8. *Nazarene Manual: 2005-2009,* 31.

9. Greathouse and Lyons, *Romans 1-8,* 238.

10. Wesley, *Works,* 5:232.

Chapter 9

1. Dillenberger, *Martin Luther,* 490.

2. *Nazarene Manual: 2005-2009,* 34-35.

3. *Sing to the Lord,* 486.

4. Ibid., 525.

5. William M. Greathouse and George Lyons, *Romans 9-16: A Commentary in the Wesleyan Tradition* (Kansas City: Beacon Hill Press of Kansas City, 2008), 129.

6. Ibid., 138.

7. Wesley, *Works,* 5:158.

8. Ibid., 7:103-4.

9. Ibid., 5:158.

10. *Book of Discipline of the United Methodist Church,* 321.

11. Wesley, *Works,* 5:169.

12. Ibid., 165-66.

Chapter 10

1. *Nazarene Manual: 2005-2009,* 242.

2. Ibid.

3. Irenaeus, *Against Heresies* 3:24:1. *The Ante-Nicene Fathers,* Vol. 1. Edited by Rev. Alexander Roberts and James Donaldson (Buffalo, N.Y.: Christian Literature Publishing, 1885).

4. Origen, *Homilies on Joshua* in *Fathers of the Church.* Edited by Cynthia White and translated by Barbara J. Bruce (Washington, D.C.: Catholic University of America Press, 2002), 50.

5. Cyprian, *Fathers of the Church,* Vol. 36. Edited by Roy J. Deferrari (New York: Fathers of the Church, 1958), 100.

6. Martin Luther, *Luther's Works,* Vol. 43. Edited by Gustavo K. Wiencke (Philadelphia: Fortress Press, 1968), 28.

7. John Calvin, *Institutes of the Christian Religion,* Vol. 2. Edited by John T. McNeill (Philadelphia: Westminster Press, 1960), 1016.

8. Schaff, *Creeds of Christendom,* 657.

9. For elaboration, see Kenneth Collins, *The Theology of John Wesley* (Nashville: Abingdon Press, 2007), 238-40.

10. Wesley, *Works,* 7:61.

11. Ibid., 5:296-97.

12. Ibid., 14:321.

13. Greathouse and Lyons, *Romans 1-8,* 131-32.

14. Wesley, *Works,* 5:187.

15. Ibid., 11:403.

16. Ibid., 7:148.

17. Ibid., 61.

18. Ibid., 11:402-3.

Chapter 11

1. Brian Kolodiejchuk, ed., *Mother Teresa: The Private Writings of the "Saint of Calcutta"* (New York: Doubleday, 2007), 271-72.

2. William M. Greathouse, *Wholeness in Christ* (Kansas City: Beacon Hill Press of Kansas City, 1998), 173.

3. Ibid., 174.

4. Ibid., 32.

5. George Maloney, ed., *Pseudo-Macarius* (New York: Paulist Press, 1992), 88-89, 134.

6. Thomas á Kempis, *The Imitation of Christ* (New York: Doubleday, 1955), 78-79.

7. Wesley, *Works,* 5:203-4.

8. Ibid., 6:413.

9. Ibid., 11:397.

Chapter 12

1. N. T. Wright, *Surprised by Hope* (New York: Harper Collins, 2008), 104.

2. Greathouse and Lyons, *Romans 9-16,* 194.

3. Wesley, *Works,* 5:184.

4. For further reading, see Mark Quanstrom, *A Century of Holiness Theology* (Kansas City: Beacon Hill Press of Kansas City, 2000).

5. *Sing to the Lord,* 521.

6. Wesley, *Works,* 5:80-81.